I Am my Father's Son

Frederick Douglas, Jr.

authorHOUSE®

AuthorHouse™
1663 Liberty Drive
Bloomington, IN 47403
www.authorhouse.com
Phone: 1 (800) 839-8640

Published by AuthorHouse 11/29/2016

ISBN: 978-1-5246-1819-3 (sc)
ISBN: 978-1-5246-1818-6 (e)

Library of Congress Control Number: 2016911598

Print information available on the last page.

Dedications

First of all, I thank God for giving me the strength and inspiration to write this book. I give Him all honor, praise and glory.

In memory of: Frederick Douglas, Sr. (12/11/1932-7/18/2004)
Yoshiko Douglas (6/20/1941-12/11/2006)
James Gill, Jr. (6/28/1933-2/17/1999)

To all my children: Lyndsey (I've never forgotten you)
Onari, Socoya, and Jeremiah

Special dedications: Cynthia Castro (sister)
The entire Gill family

I like to thank all those who stood behind me continuously giving me words of encouragement to complete this project and share this story.

Finally, to my Ruby D. who kept me focused and continually prayed for me. I couldn't have completed this without you. All I have is God-given love for you and that's forever.

Fore Thought

IT TOOK ME 46 YEARS to get to this point- to be able to finally put to rest all these spirits that have been controlling my life. I had become caught up in what the "world" wanted me to do that it turned me into a person that I didn't recognized anymore. I've become disgusted with myself and as a result, I ruined a lot of my opportunities: I became self-centered, I missed out on close friendships, I made some incredible stupid decisions, I never knew my half- sister like I should have and the worst is never getting to know a daughter I fathered. I never really had close relationships with anyone- It's a dangerous thing when you're not who you think you are- I've had become many different personalities in seeking to identify who I truly am.

The day came when I hit the lowest point of my life and it took the Grace and Mercy of God's Hand to save me from self-destruction. God had to literally trap me and counsel me with His Words- He didn't bring me this far just to let me go. God has called me to be the man that He has desired for me to be and I have accepted that calling. For that fact, we all have a calling from God that will be fulfilled, whether good or evil.

The writing of this book has been a healing process for me bringing closure on who I am and what I needed to do with my life. The most hurtful events in my life wasn't being able to say good-bye and telling my mother and father that I loved them before they both passed away. This writing was necessary to mend many wounds and bring me to the realization that I do have an identity and that God loves me. I am my father's son.

A Soldier's Poem

America will you remember us
When our bodies are lowered into the ground
We gave you our best fighting for freedom
Keeping your families safe from danger
Not letting any blood shed on our soil.

We found ourselves in a bloody battle
Men were being killed all around us
We could see the dust from enemy bombs
And the sound of machine guns firing their bullets
There was nowhere to hide or nowhere to run.

We started shooting with fear in our hearts
Listening to soldiers getting shot
A terrible feeling of death perspired on our face
As the exchange of gunfire became so intense
We were hoping that it was just a nightmare.

Seven days a week and around the clock
We were shooting to save each other's lives
Soldiers from all over gave up their souls
Fighting for your right to live in peace
Not once regretting becoming a soldier.

Bullet wounds and injuries we could not feel
As we walked for miles through a humid jungle
Looking for those that died in battle
It was an honor to carry their bodies' home
They would die again for the love of their country.

No medals of honor can replace these precious lives
They all put their country first
We were proud to serve on the battlegrounds
So remember us America we died for you
Honor us forever in your hearts.

Prologue

THIS IS A TRUE STORY based on the collection of information from U.S. Army documents, my father, Sgt. Frederick Douglas Sr., Lieutenant James N. Gill, Jr. (referred to as my uncle), and 6 other soldiers that were involved in the unauthorized mission to recover me from a Japanese black market baby ring. Army documents that my father had were also used to put together approximate timelines and fill in gaps of what might have happened during certain times where my father or uncle couldn't quite remember clearly. Some of the conversations in this story are assumptions of what might have been spoken as well as recollections from my father, uncle and a couple of men that were involved in my rescue. My father served 22 years in the U. S. Army with tours of duty in what are now Okinawa, Japan, Korea, and Viet Nam. My uncle served 20 years in the U.S. Air Force and as fate would have it, he was stationed with my father in Okinawa at Naha and Kadena Air Base between the years of 1962-1967. My father had just completed a tour of duty in Korea (3/1961-1/1962) and was being furloughed to Okinawa for a couple of months off until his next tour. It was during January of 1962 when my uncle had just arrived from the United States and was assigned between Naha Air Base and Kadena Air Force Base in charge of air tactical recon and surveillance. Actual names are used in this story for the exception of the Colonel, which I changed his name due to my father's oath of keeping him protected. What you are about to read is a father's struggle and perseverance to find his son at all cost and risk, which was a mini-war in itself.

Chapter 1

IT WAS A LATE FRIDAY morning in June of 1962 when my father, Sgt. Frederick Douglas, Sr., had arrived from a tour of duty from Korea to Naha Air Base in Okinawa. He had been wounded in the stomach area from enemy bullets, but he managed to survive until his rescue. My father was a handsome man of color standing 5'10", who had dropped out of high school to join the U.S. Army. He wanted much more in life than what was given to him at that time. He enlisted in 1948 and went through the rituals of basic training and then was assigned to the artillery battalion headed to Korea. The Army had trained him to be a weapons specialist in the first line of defense. This was to be his first time in a battle zone where he would have to kill men, women, and even children on the enemy side. It was until a few years before his death that he stopped having nightmares that would wake him in the middle of the night with sweat dripping down his face as tears clouded his eyes. My father would never talk about what had happened during those years for I could tell he was trying to blot out that part of life. My mom, who was of Japanese dissent, would always try to console him, but he would get annoyed and become argumentative. My mother started smoking cigarettes as her vice to ease her nerves extending from the many arguments and abuse that came from my father. His means of escape was his favorite bottle of Passport scotch with milk and a 6 pack of Colt 45 malt liquor beer.

I could never understand why my dad drank so much and it would always bother me when he became drunk and would start to argue with my mother, which led to sometimes him hitting her. It seemed like a demon had possessed him as he fought to control his rage. It was during these times that I would close my eyes and hide in my closet. I could hear my dad screaming, "You Jap, why the hell did I bring you here."

I must have been about 7 or 8 years old when we were living in Tampa, Florida, which was around 1970 or 1971. We lived in the River Grove subdivision on Norfolk Street, which was centrally located to Busch Gardens, Lowery Park Zoo and the historic Rogers Park golf course. This was my first experience dealing with racial tension. People would stare at my father and mother as though it was a crime for a black man to be married to a Japanese woman. I can remember getting ridiculed at school because of my multi-racial heritage. I knew that my father was probably under a lot of public scrutiny because of being the first black man to move into an all- white neighborhood with a Japanese wife and a mixed-race son. I used to get picked on to the point of becoming ashamed of my parents and who I was- a black-Japanese boy with no identity or no one to identify with. Even my father's family had a hard time initially accepting us as part of their family.

Eventually as I got older, I began to understand about race and the drift that was created between blacks and whites. I can remember my older cousin, Bryant, taking me to a white owned barbershop to get a haircut, as this became my introduction to racism. Upon entering the shop, everyone stared at us as if we were in the wrong place. One of the barbers immediately said, "I'm sorry boys, but we don't cut your kind of hair."

My cousin replied back, "What do you mean you don't cut our kind of hair?"

"Like I said, we don't cut your kind of hair."

My cousin looked around the shop and noticed that one of the barbers was cutting the hair of a blond headed white kid who had the just about the same hair texture that I had.

Pointing at the white blond headed kid, my cousin said, "His hair texture is just like my cousin- just admit that you don't want to cut his hair because we're black."

The barber replied back, "I think you boys better leave before you get in trouble."

My cousin grabbed my hand and on the way out, he muttered, "Y'all can kiss my black butt."

I was confused about the situation and didn't know what to say to my cousin. He was visibly upset and didn't say a word until we gotten back to my father's house. He told my father what had happened and my father

2

exploded as he said, "I'm going to give those crackers a piece of my mind. I gave this country over 22 years fighting for their freedom and they still call me a nigger."

My cousin grabbed my father's arm and told him to leave it alone- it would just cause problems and may get him arrested. My father eventually calmed down, but I could still tell he was still upset holding everything inside like a ticking time bomb. It was incidents like these that would drive my father to take out his frustrations on my mother and sometimes on me. Ironically, years later, that same white owned barbershop would be owned by a black man.

Chapter 2

IT WAS DURING MY HIGH school years at Hillsborough High (1979-1981) that I would begin to develop my own identity and found other groups of mixed race students that I could identify like myself. The once white neighborhood that my family moved into became pre-dominantly black. I started to accept who I was as racial tensions were limited, but still existed. I started to classify myself as being black especially after studying Black history. My father had pressured me to always consider myself as an Asian Pacific Islander as he felt that it would give me an advantage in society. I didn't have any problems interacting with any race at school- most of them thought that I was of Hispanic dissent. I found myself drawn to hanging with the "black crowd" and even dated black girls as a preference even though my father objected- his view was that I would be better off with a white girl. I felt comfortable being classified as black despite the opinions of my father.

My father had mellowed since his initial retirement from the Army. He did however, still had nightmares from time to time about the wars as he drank heavily to relieve his mind. My mother started to feel accepted by my father's family as well as by the community where we lived. My father still at times would argue with my mother, but she had learned to adjust to his ravings. There was an incident that had happened that led my father to see that I was growing up into a man. One night after my father had been drinking, he started arguing with my mother about race, finances, and her wanting to work. I was in my room talking on the phone when I heard my mother screaming. I dropped the phone and immediately ran to the living room and saw my father hitting on my mother. I jumped on his back and slid him into a headlock position squeezing his head as though I was taking years of anger and frustration out on him. I had become an evil element clamping his head trying to squeeze his brains out and refusing to let go. I could remember saying, "I'm tired of you, I'm tired of you, I wish you were dead!"

After my mother's pleading to let go, I released my father and threw him against the wall. He stared silently looking at me and I couldn't tell if he was going to cry or attack me. It would later dawn on me that the words I spoke did more damage to him than the headlock position. He continued to stare at me speechless as I picked my mother off the floor and took her to another room. I didn't know what to expect from my father, whether to fight or call the police. About a half hour had passed when I decided to take a peek at my father. It looked as though he was in a sleepy daze lying on the floor motionless. Cautiously, I approached him and asked if he was all right.

"I'm OK", he said. "Did you really mean what you said about me being dead?"

"No, I didn't mean it. I'm just tired of how you treat us sometimes and the way you just drink."

There was a brief moment of silence between us. I looked at my father's face and could see years of anguish along with the reality of his fear as tears slowly streamed from his eyes. I knew his heart was broken by what I had said and I immediately apologized.

"I didn't mean to say that-I'm sorry."

He replied back, "I'm hurt that you said that. I love you son and I never meant no harm to you or your mother."

I would never realize until my 18th birthday why my words led him to tears for the next several days afterwards.

Chapter 3

It was three days before my 18th birthday (08/01/1981), when my uncle, James Gill, had driven in from Texas to be with my family and me. It had been about 10 years since I last saw him and he had changed in appearance from the man I knew back in the day. At 6 feet tall and 180 pounds, he still looked the same for the exception of his completely bald headedness and thick blacked framed glasses. Even though he was black, his skin complexion was that of a white person and he could sometimes pass himself off as a white man when the occasion would benefit him. His loud voice would command attention even in the noisiest of rooms. Even though there wasn't any blood relation, my father has always considered him as a brother and I always knew him as my uncle. They had met in 1960 at Kadena Air Force Base in Okinawa and it was like love at first sight between the two as far as friendship. They gotten along better than their real brothers and had grown to know each other like a book. There was something natural about seeing the both of them together- a special bond that would take them to their graves.

My uncle Gill had taken a good look at my father and noticed that he had gained about 30 pounds with a pot belly- you could still see the 3 bullet wounds and the knife wound on his right side. I could never get him to talk about his wounds for I always wanted to know the stories behind them. He used hair coloring to keep the gray hairs out of his head and still wore his Brute 33 after shave which I always enjoyed the smell. He always believed in keeping himself well groomed even though he wasn't much into fashion.

"You look pregnant with that belly sticking out," my uncle said to my father.

"Sit on this", my father replied back holding up his middle finger.

I came home from a friend's house and caught my uncle by surprise.

"Well, I'll be damn if it ain't Freddie Jr. I can't believe that I'm looking at you", my uncle said as he hugged me.

I returned his hug and told him how glad I was to see him.

"It's amazing Doug that this boy is here. Look at him- all grown up." My uncle had always referred to my father as Doug.

I was pondering what my uncle meant by his comment about his amazement as to the fact that I was standing in front of him. But, that would be for later when the others arrive.

"Marco, Marco", my uncle said to my mother as she saw him.

My mother's real name was Yoshiko, but was always called Marco and till this day, I don't know how the nickname "Marco" came about.

My mother gave him a hug and welcomed him into our home.

"What you drinking brother?" my father asked my uncle.

"You know what we do man. Break out the Schlitz malt liquor" my uncle replied.

The two had were relaxing on the patio discussing old times being careful not to include me in any conversation. It was as though they were having a top-secret discussion.

My mother and I were in the kitchen preparing dinner. Like most Japanese women, my mother was very short standing at 5 feet tall, but had gained about 20 pounds to her once 120-pound stature eating American cooking. I did speak a little Japanese, but not as fluent as I once did when I was growing up in Okinawa. I would always look at pictures of my mom, dad and myself taken together- I always resembled more of my dad than my mother. My mother worked as a clerk at Naha Air Base- my mother was a beautiful young Japanese girl in her 20's when her and my dad had met. Even at her present early 40's, she still looked the same.

"Hey Freddy Jr., come out here" my uncle called for me as my mind drifted back to reality.

"Yes sir" I replied.

I went to the patio area where they were at and sat down with them.

"To celebrate your 18th birthday, we've got some peers flying into town tomorrow to help," my uncle said.

"Peers?" I asked looking puzzled.

We're all a part of your history and for your 18th birthday, we all have a story to share with you," my uncle replied. "It's very important you know them."

I was as confused as ever not knowing what to say or do. My uncle had popped open a can of beer and handed it to me. I looked at my dad for some sense of direction, but he gave no indication of what I should do about the beer.

"Come on boy, take a sip," my uncle said.

My dad finally nodded his head in approval as I took my first and last sip of what would be the most disgusting liquid I ever tasted.

"Ugh! This stuff is nasty," I said as I spat out the sip of beer.

Both my uncle and my dad started laughing.

"That's good. I don't have to worry about you being a drinker," my father said as he motioned for me to pass the beer back to him.

From that point on, I've always told myself that I would never drink or smoke in my life and I've held myself in truth to this day.

Chapter 4

ON THE DAY BEFORE MY 18th birthday, my uncle, father and I were headed inside Tampa International Airport to meet a couple of their Army/Air Force peers that served in Okinawa. My father claimed that these men played an important role in my life which I had no clue of their significance. We were waiting at the Eastern Airlines arrival gate as the plane from Dallas/Ft Worth pulled up to the ramp. It had been over 15 years since they had all seen each other and I was eager to see if they would recognize each other. My uncle Gill was an outspoken man who could strike up a conversation with any living being. He was well versed in all topics and had served in the Air Force over 20 years. He was a part of a joint armed service group, which included all members of the armed services for setting up air support for ground troops during battle. He retired to civilian life and became an air traffic controller for the FAA.

"Gill! You bald headed sonofagun," said one of the men as he strolled into the waiting area. "You still look the same."

"I be damned if it ain't Wallace Johnson. Man, you put on some pounds," my uncle replied as he gave him a bear hug and a kiss on the cheek.

Sergeant Wallace Johnson was an ammunitions expert and was a member of the Army Rangers. He was under my father's command during the Korean and Vietnam wars. He stood about 6' 2" and weighed about 250 pounds- about 50 pounds heavier from his Army days. He had thinning hair around the sides of his head with a developing bald spot on the top of his head.

"Sarge! You look good for an old man," said Sgt. Johnson to my father.

9

"Old man- who you calling old man, I got your old man," my father replied back as they gave each other a hug.

"And don't tell me that's your son. Wow! It's hard to believe that he's the one we went after."

Sgt. Johnson shook his head in amazement as he looked at me giving me a firm handshake and a hug as I wondered what he meant about me being the one they went after.

"Hey Wallace, where's Capt. Williams?" my father asked Sgt. Johnson.

My father's question got answered when a tall, lanky, white man exited the ramp tunnel. Captain Earl Williams was a member of Air Force Recon Command at Kadena Air Force Base during the 1960's and had worked with my Uncle Gill planning search and rescue missions in Korea. He had retired and became a business owner. Capt. Williams was head and shoulders above the others, as he stood up at 6'4" with a thin frame of about 180 pounds. He stretched his long arms toward my uncle Gill and gave him a rub on his head.

"Gill! I heard you all the way from the back of the crowd. Damn it's good to see all you guys. And Sarge, you look good."

"Hey Cap," said Sgt. Johnson, "Guess who this is," as he pointed toward me.

"No way- is that little Fred? I can't believe it! I would never have believed it if I didn't see him with my own eyes."

Captain Williams gave me a saluted gesture as he stretched his hand for me to shake.

"Nice to meet you sir," I said to him thinking about the mystery of all their conversations about me.

After leaving the airport, my father had taken us to MacDill Air Force Base located just outside of Tampa near Davis Islands for lunch. It was a sight to see a gathering of old soldiers talking about old times and singing the old songs of Otis Redding, James Brown, Sam Cook and The Staple Singers. My uncle was telling the story about my dad and him getting drunk one night while they were stationed at Naha- both of them had been assigned to the new artillery missile launch system, which required 2 keys to activate the missiles. They were in the missile tower drinking when my uncle had put his key to launch mode and my father had did the same. The missile launched and headed off the coast of Okinawa. To this day, neither one knows what happened with that missile nor even if the Air Force knew anything about it. The rest of the afternoon was filled with war stories, beer and liquor as they toasted to everything under the sun and even under the moon. It was a good thing I had my driver's license since my father would be in no condition to drive.

Chapter 5

I WOKE UP TO A bright early morning looking at my clock radio flashing August 1, 1981-my 18th birthday. I had expected to feel different now that I was considered a legal adult, but I didn't feel any different nor did I have the feeling that I wanted to conquer the world as most 18 year olds are eager to be on their own. My father had planned a cookout for our guests and me to celebrate my passage into manhood along with a few other surprises of one, which was a 1976 Ford Torino. But, it couldn't compare to what my uncle, father and their 2 comrades would give me.

I could hear my uncle and father in the backyard lighting the grill and talking about their plans for the day. My father swore he was a gourmet barbeque chef and his sauce should have been marketed, which it probably could have since it was that good.

"I spit in it and that's what makes it so good," my father would always say about his sauce.

My father had left my Uncle Gill and myself to watch the grill as he went to go pick up Captain Williams and Sergeant Johnson from the Admiral Benbow Inn. It was a chance for me to ask my uncle 1001 questions about the unusual gathering for my 18th birthday and what roles did Captain Williams and Sergeant Johnson have in coming to Tampa for my birthday.

"You're a special kid," my uncle spoke as he had already anticipated what questions I was going to asked him. "I just want you to know that your father and all of us here went through hell and high water for you. I can see the questions in your eyes, but you'll soon know the reason for our presence here."

"I'm just confused about why everyone keep saying that it's a miracle of some sort that I'm here and the purpose of these guys coming here for my 18th birthday," I said to my uncle as he laid the ribs and steaks on the grill.

"It's all good. What we have to tell you is a vital part of who you are and you need to know your history. Damn, you may even write a book about it one day," my uncle said not knowing that his spoken prophecy would come true.

It was around noontime when a few of my friends had arrived to help celebrate my birthday. Ivan Butcher and Miguel Monroe were two of my best friends whom I knew since middle school. We were like a band of outlaw brothers always doing something mischievous - shoplifting candy from the neighborhood store to looking at *Playboy* and *Hustler* magazines. We never did drugs, drink alcohol, or smoked cigarettes of any kind. Our conversation would always center on which girls we wanted to date or have sex- I was always the one to lure the girls and introduced them to both of my best friends. After I left for college, we all lost contact with each other and till this day, I don't have a clue as to their whereabouts.

With the song known as *Rapper's Delight* of the "Sugar Hill Gang" blasting over the stereo, my uncle Gill had shouted at me to put on some real music.

"That is real music uncle. Rap music is the new thing," I said to my uncle.

"That's not music. I'll show you real music," my uncle said as he started going through the stack of cassette tapes. "Kool and the Gang, KC and the Sunshine Band, Earth, Wind, and Fire, The Commodores- what you know about that. Y'all young dudes don't know anything about good music."

Just then, my father had arrived with Capt. Williams and Sgt. Johnson carrying bags of ice and chips.

"I heard you Gill talking about real music. Don't forget the Eagles, the Steve Miller Band, Rod Stewart, and Elton John or even Kiss," said Capt. Williams as he grinned at my uncle.

"Yeah, they were some funky white boys too," my uncle replied.

All four men were gathered around the grill as they were going back and forth about the whereabouts of the other men in their unit. My two friends were tending to the music while I was in the kitchen helping my mother with the potato salad. She was always very protective of me during the early childhood years and would always tell me stories of Japanese culture and traditions so I wouldn't forget that part of my heritage. Even though she spoke English well, she would always speak to me in Japanese and I would try to answer her back the same. A family portrait hung in the living room, which I would always look at- my mother was a beautiful young Japanese woman in her young 20's when my father first met her in Okinawa. They never spoke, but just smiled lightly at each other- at that time, it was not customary for Japanese women to interact with American soldiers. My father never went into detail about how he finally ended up marrying my mother nor would my mother share her story of how the both of them got together. But nonetheless, I was happy that my mother and father got married for I wouldn't be celebrating my 18th birthday on this day or so I thought.

Chapter 6

It was well into the afternoon as the 3 o'clock sun started its dissent, as the smell of barbeque filled the air along with the sounds of the 70's soul music. All of us were eating like there was no tomorrow leaving anything but bare bones from the ribs and chicken. As usual, my father did his thing with the sauce and my mother's potato salad and egg rolls would make you slap someone's grandmother.

"Damn, this is got to be the best barbeque I've ate," said Capt. Williams, as he was showing no shame in licking his fingers. "I need the secret to the sauce and the stuffed egg rolls."

"You can forget about the sauce. Doug ain't giving it up on the sauce. Marco may give you the recipe for the egg rolls," my uncle had replied.

After everyone had finished eating, my mother brought out a birthday cake with 18-lit candles as everyone sang "Happy Birthday" in unison focusing their eyes on me.

"Blow out the candles and make a wish," my uncle shouted to me.

I felt awkward. The last time I blew out candles on a birthday cake was on my 10th birthday. I quickly closed my eyes, made a wish, and then blew out the candles. Everyone started clapping as they gave me high five's and shook my hand.

"I would've never thought that I would see this day," Capt. Williams said. "I'm just sorry that the others couldn't be here. It would've been great to see their faces."

"You got that right," added Sgt. Johnson. "I would've love to see their faces."

My uncle, seeing the confusion on my face as to the conversation taking place, picked up the conservation.

"We had planned this day 15 years ago back in Okinawa. We all agreed to reunite on your 18th birthday to share this day with you, but unfortunately, we couldn't find Smitty, Roland, or Favors. Colonel Boyd and 3 others passed away several years ago."

I had no idea what my uncle was talking about, but soon, I would find out that all these men would become a permanent part of my life history. My father had brought out a bottle of champagne as he poured a glass for everyone.

"A toast to my son. I am proud of you and all that you have accomplished thus far. May you live well and remember us," my father said as he held up his glass and motioned everyone to touch glasses.

"Thank you all for making this a great birthday," I said after sipping my champagne.

"Happy Birthday," my father said as he threw me a set of keys with strands of ribbon tied around it.

"Oh man!" I said as I took a moment to examine the "Ford" labeled keys. "How you know I wanted a Mustang." I had already knew that the keys belonged to a 1976 Ford Torino- I had overheard my father telling my mom that he had purchased the car from an Air Force pilot going overseas a week before my birthday.

"Well, it's not exactly a Mustang, but it is sporty. It looks like the "Starsky and Hutch" Torino," my father replied back. "We'll have to pick it up tomorrow from the detail shop."

I had counted up about a thousand dollars in hundred dollar bills that came in an envelope signed by Capt. Williams, Sgt. Johnson, my uncle Gill, and my mother, which was my birthday gift from them. My two best friends looked in awed as they motioned to me to look at the cash.

"You lucky dog!" Miguel said as he counted the bills. "How about giving me a hundred?"

"Yeah right!" I replied back. "This money is going into the bank. I'll need it when I go off to school."

"Go ahead and spend some of it. You and your buddies can hook up with some girls and take them out when you get your car tomorrow,' my father said.

"Sounds like a plan to me," Ivan said as he high-fived my other best friend, Miguel.

I nodded my head in agreement as I took a hundred dollars out of the envelope and gave the rest to my mother to keep. I had already knew who I was going to ask to go out with me- the only problem was getting dates for my two best friends, which wouldn't be hard since I was paying for everything.

The evening sun was starting to disappear as the time on my watch flashed eight o' clock. Everyone pitched in cleaning the backyard as the music of the Temptations played in the background. My party had turned out better than expected- I was glad that all my father's friends came- especially when they all gave me a thousand dollars. My two best friends hugged me as they were leaving to go home anticipating our dates for the following evening.

"Call us when you have everything set up and let us know what time to get ready," Miguel said as he threw me a Tootsie Roll candy.

"I'll call you guys in the afternoon. Thanks for coming," I replied back.

I was in the kitchen helping my mother with the remaining dishes and putting up the leftover food. Everyone else was outside sitting in the lounge chairs talking about more old times. I thanked my mother for her part in making my birthday a success and that I was going to take her to our favorite Japanese restaurant for lunch the next day.

"Hey Freddie Jr.," my uncle called me as I turned my attention toward the backyard. "Come join us."

"Coming," I said as I gave my mother a kiss on the cheek.

All eyes were on me as I approached the group sitting outside. 'Have a seat," my uncle said. "We all got one more surprise for you. It's not really a surprise, but its some things about your life you need to know."

"Now that you're 18 Freddie Jr., we all have something to share with you that will explain a lot of things about your life," my uncle said as he looked me in the eyes.

I looked back at my uncle not knowing whether to expect something great or something awful. I looked at my father, but all he could muster up was a blank stare into the nighttime clouds as if he was afraid of what was about to be spoken.

"We all waited a long time to come see you on this day," my uncle said as he motioned for me to sit next to him. "You know, your father and

I planned this day back in Okinawa and we all agreed that on your 18th birthday, we would reveal some things you need to know."

I gave a puzzled look at the men in the group trying to figure out what they were about to tell me.

"I don't understand," I said.

"Oh, you will," my uncle replied back.

I had figured that they were going to tell me about being a man and facing life's challenges and all that B.S. that goes along with it. Boy was I wrong- what would be spoken to me would be a total shocker.

Chapter 7

My Uncle Gill was well versed in almost all topics from politics, sports, religion and world news. He had been with the United States Air Force for over 20 years and seen a lot of life changing events that affected our country. He was part of a joint armed services group, which included members of the Army, Marines and Navy personnel responsible for setting up air support for ground combat troops during battle. It was during this time that my uncle and father first met and from that time on till their deaths, they became brothers separated only by blood. They would be stationed together for most of their military service careers. He retired to a civilian life in 1972 and continued his service for the government as an air traffic controller for the FAA.

"You're a special kid," my uncle started as he sipped on a cold can of Colt 45. "It all started back in September of 1962, when your father and I were stationed in Okinawa at Naha Air Base."

I can remember my father telling me a brief history of Okinawa, which is an island of Japan located in the North Pacific Ocean, about 350 miles south of Kyushu, Japan's southernmost main island. Okinawa is the largest of the Ryukyu Islands, which are a Japanese prefecture. Naha is the island's chief town and port. The United States Government had retained Okinawa during WWII.

Naha Airfield was a wartime Imperial Japanese facility until the United States Government seized it during the Battle of Okinawa on April 1, 1945. After the war, it became a major United States Air Force installation known as Naha Air Base. Fishing was the way of life for most Okinawans and the villages depended heavily on the economic support from the military base. Many of the military personnel would purchase merchandise and foods as well as eating at some of the sushi and sake bars. But, there were certain parts of Okinawa that was considered unsafe, mostly inhabited by "war gangs"- one wouldn't be caught in that part of Okinawa unless you had a business arrangement with someone. Also, Okinawans held the distinction for having the most people over a hundred years old, which they still maintain that distinction today.

"Your dad and I had just come back from our first tour of duty from Korea," my uncle continued. "It was June of 1961 or was it later than that Doug?"

"It was about that time," my father replied. "We were at Kadena Base before being sent to Naha."

My father and uncle had returned from combat in Korea. My father had received gunshot wounds to his stomach and had minor surgery.

"That's right," my uncle said. "Your father had left the hospital a few days after his surgery and had a desperate taste for some sake and yakisoba."

Saki is a wine made from rice and yakisoba is a fried noodle dish with veggies and meat added if desired.

My uncle adjusted his thick black-framed glasses as he continued talking. "We went to our usual spot outside the base that we frequented almost every day. Miss Tomiko was the owner and she knew exactly what to prepare for us when she saw us enter through the doors."

"Konichiwa. Have seat, I fix for you now," Miss Tomiko would always say as my uncle tried to imitate how she sounded.

My father was reminiscing about how good the food had been. My uncle nodded in agreement as he added that the sake wasn't so bad either.

Capt. Williams and Sergeant Johnson both laughed as my uncle started singing the "sake" song in a drunken fashion- the "sake" song was a song of the winos sung to the tune of London Bridge.

"Heck Doug, you drank more sake than anybody. They started calling you Sake Doug," my uncle said laughing heartily. "Well anyway, your father saw this lady walking in carrying baskets of fruit. He got up to go help her unload some of her baskets. She thanked him and he replied back in Japanese with you're welcome beautiful lady."

My father and uncle were semi- fluent in the Japanese language and were able to communicate effectively. Most Okinawans knew English well enough to handle business transactions, but more often, my father would always serve as a translator for most American soldiers conducting business in the village.

"Your father took a liking to this little Japanese woman and invited her to sit with us. She was kind of shy, but she accepted his invitation."

My uncle went into detail describing how the lunch went with the three of them.

My father said that her name was Mitsuko and she was a merchant at one of the markets in the village. She sold fabric for making kimonos as well as kimono dolls. She was about 5'3" tall and thin as most Okinawan women were small in stature. Mitsuko was attractive and humble towards my father. They started dating for a few months when she ended up getting pregnant, which wasn't supposed to happen- Mitsuko told my father that she couldn't have children. I was shocked that my father didn't tell me that I possibly had a half brother or sister somewhere in Japan.

"I told Doug that something sounded "fishy" to me and that I didn't like how Mitsuko would always be secretive as to her family background and had an evil eye toward me when I questioned her," my uncle said as he threw a quick glance toward my father. "She was about 8 months pregnant when your father asks her to marry him, which she quickly accepted. But, I knew that something wasn't right and I told Doug that he shouldn't be quick to marry her. As always, your father was stubborn and I ended up being the best man when they got married."

Mitsuko and my father were married on July 1, 1963. I started to get confused trying to figure out how my mother, Yoshiko, fitted into all this- I thought how my father could be married to Mitsuko when I thought he was married to my mother. Eventually, I found out that my father was married to Mitsuko before he met my mother.

My uncle looked at my father and asked if he wanted to pick up the conversation.

"No, you're doing well. Go ahead," my father replied.

Capt. Williams and Sergeant Johnson were listening as though they were waiting for the next scene to unfold, trying to figure out what was going to happen. I looked at my father and he seemed to feel a little uncomfortable as my uncle started to get deeper into his story.

"Well, about a month after they were married, Mitsuko gave birth to a baby boy. I was the first at the hospital to see the baby and he resembled Mitsuko."

My uncle threw a glance at my father as to signal him to say something. Meanwhile, I thought about what my uncle was telling me- it made no sense to me why he was telling me this story.

"Never thought I would see this day," my uncle said as he took a swallow of his Colt 45.

"What do you mean uncle?" I asked.

Oh, just thinking out loud."

After swallowing the last of his beer, my father went into the house and a few minutes later, came back with a large brown envelope. He handed the envelope to me and told me to take everything out.

"What's all this," I asked, as I took out a collection of pictures and documents.

I saw a picture of a lady holding a newborn baby. I figured that the lady was Mitsuko holding my father's child. My father confirmed my thoughts about the picture.

"That's Mitsuko," my father said after taking a deep breath. "And the baby she's holding is you."

Chapter 8

THERE WAS A MOMENT OF silence as my eyes were fixated on the picture of this woman who was supposed to be my mother. I looked through the patio window gazing at my mother in the kitchen. She was the only mother that I ever knew and I couldn't think otherwise.

"How could this woman in this picture be my mother," I thought to myself.

I looked at my mother again as she was putting away leftover food, trying to draw any resemblance to the woman in the picture hoping that she was the same woman. The only mother I knew had long black hair with a round face and long eyelashes. The woman in the picture had short black hair with an oval face.

"How can this be," I said looking at the picture. "I don't remember this woman as my mother."

My Uncle Gill and my father remained silent. My uncle retrieved a cigar from his pocket and began to smoke as my father went in the house to grab a few more beers for everyone sitting outside. Capt. Williams and Sergeant Johnson continued to look over more pictures and documents trying to piece together the story that was unfolding. I looked at my mother discussing something with my father as my mind pondered back through the years of my childhood. As early as 3 years old, I remembered my mother walking me to the school bus for the first time. She was there for all of my "first steps" and took care of me while my father went away to combat. There were plenty of pictures in our family album to validate that she, Yoshiko Douglas, was my mother and not this woman in the picture. I became angry that my father would allow this imposter in the picture to claim me as her son. If it hadn't been for my uncle calling my name, I would have ripped that picture into pieces.

"Freddy, you all right?" my uncle asked me.

I looked at him and shrugged my shoulders.

"I know it's hard to believe, but you have to know the whole story. There's a whole lot more."

"What else more could there be?" I asked my uncle as he motioned toward Capt. Williams to hand him a beer.

"There's more and we haven't even got to where Wallace, Earl and the rest of the gang fit in the story," my uncle replied back.

I started pulling out other pictures of this woman along with documents proving that she was indeed my birth mother. The birth certificate issued from the Army hospital showed her name, Mitsuko Douglas, as my birth mother along with my father's name. It showed my date of birth as August 1, 1963. There was also a marriage certificate showing that my father and this woman, Mitsuko, were married on July 1, 1963, a month before I was born. Another document showed a certificate of divorce along with pages of military documents from what looked like court proceedings showing that I am my father's son. There were also Japanese written documents, which I couldn't understand, but my father later told me that these documents gave him approval to marry Yoshiko and claim me as her son. I was confused and amazed at the same time wondering what all this meant. It seemed like hours had passed when my father came back with more beers and my uncle had finished smoking his cigar.

"Your father and I went through a lot to get you," my uncle said. "I told your father that when you turned 18, we needed to tell you everything."

My father nodded his head in agreement as he spoke, "I tried to keep this from you, but I couldn't go to my grave without you knowing your history."

"You mean to tell me there's more to it than Mitsuko?" I asked.

"Yeah, a lot more," my father replied. "It was a war in itself to get you."

"What could they possibly be talking about- what did he mean it was a war in itself to get me?" I thought to myself, looking at the four men before my eyes.

My mother had brought some snacks that she had prepared in the kitchen. Fried tempura and rice wrapped in seaweed was of my father and uncle's favorite foods. I could sense that my mother knew of the conversation taking place, as she didn't know how to react to me when handing me my plate. I got up to give my mother a hug and told her that I loved her. She felt somewhat relieved at me saying that to her. After serving the snacks, she went back into kitchen as she threw a smiling glance at my father. After we had finished eating, my father pop opened another can of beer and motioned to the others to do the same.

"What do you think so far?" my uncle asked me.

"I'm still stunned, but I'm waiting to see what more could there be," I replied back.

"Well, for one thing, you do have brothers and sisters in Okinawa from Mitsuko's other marriage," my father said.

"Is Mitsuko still alive?" I asked.

"I assume she's still alive. She would be in her mid-50's."

"Yeah, after we left Okinawa in '68, that was the last we saw of her," my uncle added.

Chapter 9

I WAS BORN ON AUGUST 1, 1963, at Naha Army Hospital in Okinawa. My father and uncle were both present at my birth observing through a glass window while my birth mother, Mitsuko, was pushing me out. My father said that I came out silently surrounded by a peaceful glow. My father had longed to have a son since he had a daughter back in the states, who I would meet at a later time in life. My uncle said that I looked more Japanese at birth than I would at any other part of my life. Mitsuko held me in her arms momentarily while the doctors finished their procedures. She took to me and said in Japanese that she would never let me go.

"Well Doug, you got yourself a son," my uncle said proudly.

"Oh yeah, isn't he a sight," my father replied back.

After the doctor had finished their procedures with Mitsuko, one of the nurses brought me to the observation window for my father and uncle to see how I looked. The nurse had instructed my father to wash his hands and put on a cap and gown, which he did, and entered into the observation room. The nurse handed me to my father.

"Behold, Frederick Douglas, Jr.," my father said.

"Damn Doug, fine looking boy," my uncle replied from the other side of the window.

My father held me under the light observing all my body parts and in the process, noticed that I had a birthmark underneath my left shoulder like him.

"He seems healthy to me- he's got all his fingers and toes," my father said.

Mitsuko was taken to a recovery room while I was taken to the nursery for further routine examination. My father had followed me to the nursery to get another glimpse of me. My uncle said that my father broke out in tears thanking some supreme being for my birth.

Mitsuko had recovered well from giving birth and was walking around the hospital ward. My father and she were discussing plans for the future concerning the family. My father was to be deployed back to Korea in 30 days and the plan was for Mitsuko and me to stay on Base until his return and then, moved to the United States- it would be a big move for Mitsuko to leave behind her family.

After spending 3 days at the hospital, my father had to attend a weeklong deployment meeting discussing strategic plans and troop movement for Korea at Kadena Air Force Base. My uncle would also be in attendance as a support for Air Tactic Command, but he would remain, leaving my father to return by himself. It was during this week that life would change for my father, uncle, and me.

Chapter 10

MY FATHER HAD RETURNED FROM his deployment meetings and was anxious to get to the hospital to see Mitsuko and me. My uncle had to fly to Tokyo to meet with some buddies from the Marines that he knew from Texas. My father had arrived at the hospital and proceeded to the ward where Mitsuko was staying. Upon entering her room, he noticed that the beds were empty and no personal belongings were in the room.

"Maybe they moved her to another room," my father thought to himself.

My father went to the nursery to see if he could find me, but I too was gone. He stopped one of the nurses to question her on our whereabouts.

"Excuse me, do you know where I can find Mitsuko Douglas and the baby Douglas?"

Yes sir, Mitsuko and the baby were discharged about 2 days ago. I believe a family member took her and the baby home," the nurse replied.

My father had a puzzled look on his face for he had really never met any of Mitsuko's family for they were against her marrying my father and didn't want anything to do with him.

"Do you know who picked them up?"

"I believe it was her brother."

"Are you sure?"

"Let me check the records and I'll let you know for sure," the nurse said as she proceeded to the nurse's station.

My father started to become nervous about the scene that was taking place. He had no clue where Mitsuko would have gone if she weren't at home.

28

"Sergeant Douglas, according to our records, your wife checked out on August 6th and she left with her brother," the nurse said. "That was 2 days ago."

"Her who?" asked my father, looking dumfounded.

"Her brother."

My father started remembering conversations that he had with Mitsuko while they were dating and she mentioned that she had 4 sisters, but no brothers. She never gave any details about her family and told my father that she lived on the outskirts of the village.

"Where could she possibly be and who is this so called brother?" my father thought frantically to himself.

My father immediately left the hospital and headed toward the housing complex where Mitsuko and he lived. As he entered the house, there was no sign of Mitsuko as he searched each room. Her clothes were still in the closet and everything was still left untouched since he had left for his deployment meetings.

"Where the hell could they be at?" he asked himself.

My father sat on the couch with his head in his hands thinking of where Mitsuko could have gone, but more importantly, where was his son. She never mentioned anything specific about where her family lived or who were her friends. My father fumbled around his pocket, looking for the phone number that my uncle had given him to contact while he was in Tokyo. He could barely dial the numbers as panic set in on him.

"Gill, Mitsuko and the baby are gone!"

"What the hell you mean Doug?"

"I think something happened to them. I don't know where they're at."

My father went on to explain what happened at the hospital telling my uncle what the nurse had told him and that there was no sign of Mitsuko ever being at home.

"I think you're over reacting Doug. Maybe she went to her family to let them see the baby. She'll probably return in a few days, after all, she knew we were going to be away for a few days."

"I don't think so. Mitsuko would have let me known or left a message if she was going to do that."

My father and uncle agreed to wait a day or two to see if Mitsuko and I would come back home before pursuing any further action.

Chapter 11

A COUPLE OF DAYS HAD passed and Mitsuko never showed up. My father knew something had to be done rather quickly to find his wife and son. He could file a missing persons report with the military police, but he knew that it wouldn't probably do any good since their jurisdiction didn't go beyond the military gates. Mitsuko and I were no longer on U.S. government soil and were protected under the Japanese government. The Okinawan police wasn't really set up to look for missing persons and even if they could, it would be weeks before they would start searching- weeks that my father didn't have, for my father would be deployed to Korea in 5 days.

"Damn, this is some messed up bull," he said to himself. "Where is my family?"

It would now be virtually impossible to locate us especially if we were on the mainland of Japan. Besides, the Japanese and U.S. governments wouldn't allow my father to take me back without having to go through the bureaucracy of both governments, which at the time, wasn't feasible.

The ringing of the phone interrupted my father's thoughts as he desperately hoped that it was someone calling with news of Mitsuko and me.

"Hey Doug, any word yet on Freddie Jr." my uncle asked on the other end.

"No, nothing. I think we have a major problem on our hands."

"That don't sound good Doug," my uncle replied. "Meet me at the NCO club in 30 minutes."

The NCO club (non-commissioned officers) was the setting for lunch as my father and uncle discussed what could have happened to Mitsuko and me.

30

"Alright Doug, what the hell happened?"

"I think Mitsuko took the baby and ran away. The hospital said some man who claimed to be her brother picked her up."

"Any idea where they may be at?"

"I have some areas where we can look, but it may be a little dangerous."

My father had remembered that Mitsuko said something about having some relatives in Nagoya, which is a major port city in Japan, located about 850 miles from Okinawa.

"It's a long shot, but they could be in Nagoya," my father had mentioned to my uncle.

"I don't think they would have gone there. You're talking about 3 days of travel to get there. I say we search the villages outside the base- maybe someone saw them."

"Yeah, I guess so. Maybe someone did see them," my father responded.

With only 5 days left to my father's deployment, he knew that a lot of ground had to be covered and it would take the both of them searching around the clock. The hospital had taken pictures of Mitsuko and me when I was born, which my father had copies of the pictures made for getting some sort of lead with the natives. This would be dangerous for both my father and uncle to do since they would be searching on their own without the approval of base command or the Okinawan police. Any broken laws of the Japanese government would result in serious repercussions for both.

'We could get in a lot of trouble for this," my uncle said.

"I want my son and I don't care what I have to do to get him back," replied my father. "You don't have to come Gill. You shouldn't have to jeopardize your career for me."

"Hell Doug, if the shoe was on the other foot, I'd probably do the same thing."

My father and uncle left the NCO club and headed back to my uncle's apartment to outline their plans for the search. My uncle knew the territories of Okinawa and suggested that they start outside the main gate and work their way into the village and beyond. The next four days and nights would be intensive with no time for sleep. My father's unit was to be deployed on the coming Saturday and he was determined to find me.

"Let's load up the guns and get some sleep. We'll leave early in the morning before daybreak," my uncle said.

Listen To My Father's Voice

I can remember riding with my father in his car
listening to the sounds of the old days
driving to the store pass the neighborhood bar
admiring a man set in his ways

He was a quiet man who was in pain
who had just come back from fighting America's war
the shooting of guns drove him insane
bombs exploding like a lion's roar

He would cry out in the middle of the night
with nightmares of killing a young child
would he be able to survive such a sight
only a drink of gin could keep him mellow and mild

He could never forgive himself for that fear
even though his country honored him for it
only God could wipe away his anguished tear
and save him from the depts of hell's pit

With the enemy and death riding on his heel
he carried his wounded fellow soldier for miles
wondering how anyone couldn't possibly feel
the demonic eyes and bitter smiles

He managed to escape even though he was shot
saving as many soldiers along the way
not even thinking if he would die and rot
as long as freedom would see the light of day

Many medals would be worn on his chest
but none could bring comfort to his broken heart
or bring him to a place of peaceful rest
yes America, my father did his part

Now listen to the suffering in his voice
for this would be his final night
no more shall he feel pain, but rejoice
for God has taken up his fight.

Chapter 12

IT WAS GETTING LATE INTO the evening as everyone started yawning from the activities of the day. My father had asked if they wanted to meet in the morning and continue with the story.

"Hey, I'm alright," Capt. Williams said as he let out a mountainous yawn. "In fact, I'm caught up into it and waiting to see where our part comes."

"I'm good too," Sgt. Johnson added.

"If you're good with it Gill, we can continue," my father said.

"I'm good. But, what about Freddy Jr?" replied my uncle.

"I'm fine. I don't think I can sleep anyway," I said to my father and uncle.

"Alright then, I guess we can continue, but I'm done with these Colt 45's," my father said as he motioned for my uncle to continue with the story.

It was early Tuesday morning around 4 a.m. when my father and uncle had awakened and completed double checking everything they needed for their search. Once everything was confirmed, they took off in their jeep and headed toward the outskirts of the main base entrance. My father had copies of pictures of Mitsuko and me taken at the hospital to show around along with American money for "buying" information. Okinawans knew the value of the American dollar and hopefully information leading to Mitsuko and I could be exchanged for it.

The morning sun was making its entrance as the sound of a nearby rooster could be heard as the markets and restaurants were opening for business. My father and uncle stopped at their usual eating place where Miss Tomiko was cooking fish. She was shocked to see the both of them so early in the morning.

"Why you here so early- I have no yakisoba for you," Miss Tomiko said.

"No, Miss Tomiko, we're not here to eat. We need some information," my father replied back in Japanese.

My father removed a picture of Mitsuko and me from his jacket and showed it to Miss Tomiko.

"You know who this lady with baby?" my father asked Miss Tomiko in Japanese.

"I know lady- she worked at fabric shop down the street. But, I no see her in a long time. Never see baby either," Miss Tomiko replied back in Japanese.

Miss Tomiko stared at the picture for a moment longer as if she was trying to figure out the resemblance of the baby. Looking at my birth pictures, I had no resemblance to my father and looked more like Mitsuko.

My father thanked Miss Tomiko and my father and uncle left the restaurant. That scene would be the same for the entire day- there were some that recognized Mitsuko, but had no clue as to her whereabouts. However, the owner of the fabric shop where Mitsuko worked at, gave my father an address of a home off the marketplace road, but found the house to be abandoned. They had spent the entire day questioning everyone they came in contact with, but no one could offer any information, even with showing of American money. It was getting dark as frustration settled in my father's voice.

"I can't believe no one has seen them. Something has to turn up quick- we got less than 72 hours."

My uncle remained silent, for he knew there was nothing he could say to ease my father's mind.

"We might as well pack it up and head toward Shuri. We can campout there and check with the natives in the morning," my uncle said after a few minutes of silence.

After driving several miles, they came upon a flat area to camp for the night.

"We'll get breakfast early in the morning. We'll find them," my uncle said as he tried to offer words of encouragement to my father.

My father tossed and turned most of the night thinking about the horrid possibility of having to leave me behind and never seeing me again.

He replayed all the conversations that Mitsuko and he ever had searching for any locations that she might have spoken. She never mentioned anything about her family or personal life to my father. He never met anyone from her family- the only thing he knew was what she told him about her family despising her for marrying a Black-American soldier. This was her reason for not bringing my father around her family.

"Got to be something somewhere," my father thought to himself. He couldn't bring anything into remembrance that would aid in his search.

A loud bell ringing nearby woke my father and uncle around 5:30 am. After quickly changing themselves and cleaning their camp, they headed toward the waterfront village of Shuri hoping for better luck. The villagers weren't as friendly with American soldiers and sometimes would refuse to service them in certain establishments. There was fishing boats docked everywhere as most of the villagers worked and lived in their boats. There were a few markets opened with merchants selling their goods while others were setting up their displays. The smell of fish and rice from one of the shops caught the attention of my father and uncle.

"That fish smells good," my father said. "It's coming from over there," as he pointed in the direction of the shop where the smell was coming from.

"Yeah, time to chow down," my uncle replied.

The owner of the establishment was about to refuse service to my father and uncle until he saw the handful of dollar bills that were in my uncle's hand.

While they were waiting for their food to be served, my father was observing the Wednesday morning sunrise wondering if he would ever see me again. He buried his face in his hands as his mind drifted back to the hospital nursery where he had first held me in his arms. For the first time in many years, he genuinely smiled toward the sun and gave God thanks.

The clanging of the plates on their table by the cook brought my father back to reality. My father pulled out the picture of Mitsuko and me and showed it to the cook.

"You know this woman?" my father asked the cook in Japanese.

The cook was ignoring the picture until my father placed a dollar bill in his hands. The cook held the picture up close and studied it for a moment.

"Sorry, I don't know woman. I wish I could help since you pay," said the cook in Japanese.

"Doesn't look good Gill," my father said as he barely touched his food.

"Realistically, we need an entire search team for this," my uncle replied. "It's not over yet- we still got a couple of more days to look."

They both departed the restaurant and spent the rest of the day scouring the entire village by foot showing pictures of Mitsuko and me, but no one knew of us. They even got jilted out of a few dollars as one of the natives gave them a fake address to where Mitsuko may have been.

"We might as well check the mountain country- it'll take a couple of days to search the villages there," my uncle said.

The next couple of days would be a great disappointment for my father and uncle, as they would receive the same response from everyone- that they didn't know the woman in the picture or the baby. Friday had come quickly and the realization of never seeing me again started to dawn on my father's mind as they headed back toward Naha. My father's unit would be deployed to Korea in 24 hours.

Chapter 13

IT WAS EARLY SATURDAY MORNING, hours before the deployment of my father's unit, as he went to see the senior officer of the Army of Naha Base.

"Permission to speak sir," said my father to Colonel Stephen Boyd, who was in charge of the Army ground support and one of the base commanders. "I need to talk to you off the record."

Col. Boyd was a big supporter and fan of my father- my father led the Army boxing team to several armed forces championships and trained Col. Boyd as a boxer years earlier, as they had become good friends.

"Alright Doug, what's on your mind?"

"I need to skip this rotation to Korea."

"You know that's impossible Doug. Your unit is being shipped out today- besides, you're their leader. What excuse in God's creation would make you request such a thing?"

My father went on to explain his dilemma about having to find Mitsuko and me and that if he waited until his return from Korea, it would be impossible to find us.

Col. Boyd had sympathized with my father, but knew that there was no way Army Central Command would approve such a request on short notice. He told my father that trying to find Mitsuko and me would be like trying to find a needle in a haystack- that we could be anywhere.

"I hate to say it Doug, but I don't think you'll ever see them again. And even if you did locate them on Japanese soil, the Japanese government wouldn't allow you to take him from his mother. Our relationship with the Japanese is so sensitive at the moment that we don't need any issues that will cause friction."

My father knew that Col. Boyd was speaking the truth, but deep down inside, he wouldn't give up. He left the Colonel's office and headed to his battalion briefing to review deployment orders with his unit. All he could think about was his son and that he would never get to see me again.

"Sgt. Douglas," shouted a voice from the back of the building. It was my uncle calling as he worked his way through the crowd of soldiers to where my father was standing. "I just found out that I'm staying here with Air Command to coordinate air support for your unit. I won't be going to Korea."

"No bull," my father replied. "Then promise me Gill that you'll continue to search for my son."

My uncle knew that this was an impossible request, but he agreed to it for my father's peace of mind.

"Don't get your hopes up Doug. I'll keep looking, but you know like I know, he may be gone for good."

Later that evening, my father's unit had shipped out to Korea for 10 months of ground artillery support, which at times would produce some bloody fights. Not a day would pass without my father thinking of me. Night after night, he replayed many scenes trying to remember anything that Mitsuko might have said to give him any clues as to our whereabouts.

The following is my father's account along with Sgt. Johnson of their experiences in battle:

"Soon after my platoon landed in Korea, we found ourselves in the middle of a bloody battle. Men were being killed and wounded all around us. I could see the dust kicked up by the impact of enemy bullets hitting the ground. There was no shelter other than a few bushes as my men and I started shooting- it became horrific to the point that I thought we were going to die with nowhere to hide. We dug holes in the ground as our only means of providing some sort of cover from the enemy. Seven days a week and around the clock we exchanged gunfire with the enemy from these holes in the ground that quickly turned into mud pits when it rained. It was unbearably cold at night and in such holes we ate and slept.

Our search and destroy missions took us in and out of the humid wooded areas with the ever-present danger of the enemy jumping out of the underbrush of leaves and fallen trees. At times, for hours on end, we were under constant pounding of artillery exploding around us. I became a killing machine, shooting men, women and children on the enemy side, as dirt roads became filled with corpses. Suddenly, the fighting stopped and I survived, but I cannot say the same for the men I carried back to camp. I can remember carrying one of men who was wounded very badly- I was holding his intestines in my hands where shrapnel from an artillery blast had punctured his stomach area. He said to me, "Sgt., just let me die here- I'm not going to make it." I told him to live and that was an order as I carried him 10 miles back to camp where he died in my arms. I clutched him tightly and cried. The medals I received from my country couldn't replace the young men I lost in battle, the men, women, and children I killed, and possibly the son that I would never see again."

Sgt, Johnson had concluded that after 10 months in Korea, 118 soldiers from their unit gave their lives to a ruthless war along with the many that were wounded. To this day, they still carry the scars and emotions of that war- even time couldn't heal their pain.

Chapter 14

AFTER 10 MONTHS OF WAR in Korea, my father's platoon received orders to rotate back to Okinawa. My father was anxious to talk to my uncle about any progress in obtaining information as to my whereabouts. He knew that the odds were greatly against him of ever finding me after a year's time. As the C-130 transport plane was near Naha, my father looked out through the window overlooking the mountains and villages wondering if I could be anywhere in them. Realizing the environment of the landscape, my father nearly convinced himself that he would be returning to the U.S. without his son.

As the troops were exiting the plane, my uncle along with a host of staff officers greeted my father and his platoon. After all the formalities were exchanged, my Uncle Gill knew that my father would have a ton of questions to ask him concerning Mitsuko and me. During the course of the war, my uncle couldn't put a lot of effort into sustaining a consistent search for me due to him being one of key personnel of the air recon support team, which required him to be on base majority of the time. Whenever he had the opportunity, my uncle circulated pictures of Mitsuko and me to the merchants and other service personnel going to the Japanese mainland, but no one had come forth with any information.

"Glad to see you're alive and well," my uncle said as he hugged my father.

"Glad to see you too," my father replied as he rubbed my uncle's freshly shaved head.

My father and uncle exchanged conversations about the war in Korea and everything that happened with their respective units. My uncle was trying very hard to keep the conversation from shifting to Mitsuko and me. My father could sense that my uncle didn't have anything good to say about us. He let the conversation stay on the war for the rest of that day.

My father and his platoon spent a couple weeks in the hospital for examinations and de-briefing. It was discovered that my father had sustained a minor bullet wound in his stomach area, which he didn't noticed- he thought he was having cramps from indigestion due to eating insects and plants during the war. After the examinations and de-briefings were completed, my uncle had planned a surprise party for my father and his platoon at the NCO club. My uncle had thought that this would be a good thing to do to ease tensions between the two as well as take my father's mind off the recent war in Korea.

The following is my Uncle Gill's account of what happened:

"Even though he didn't express it, I knew that Doug was upset that I couldn't do anything more to obtain information on the whereabouts of Mitsuko and Freddie Jr. After Doug's departure for Korea, I knew that chances were slim to none that they would never be found. I gave up all hope after months went by with no information coming forth from the pictures that I distributed. I admit, I threw in the towel and didn't put forth any efforts after the first three months. It was hard to juggle handling my duties on base and spending off time searching for Mitsuko and Freddie Jr. It would have taken an army of our own to handle such a task searching for them and even that would pose major problems with the U.S. and Japanese governments giving us permission to do such a search. Anyway, I had planned the party to take Doug's mind off of them- he had approached me during the party and told me that he didn't blame me or was he angry with me for not being able to do anything. We spent the rest of the evening getting stoned drunk."

Both drunk as can be, my father and uncle somehow managed to make their way back to their housing complex. They were sitting on the curb of the street singing songs in Japanese and English, which wouldn't make sense to someone listening- one would laugh hysterically as if they were watching a live comical sketch. A couple of military police officers, one who knew both my father and uncle, assisted them inside my father's apartment and laid them both on the couch. A short time later, my father felt sick and threw up on my uncle and on the couch where they were sitting. My father would later say that he felt his entire stomach come through his throat. My uncle didn't even move- he laid in vomit until the next morning. My father lay motionless on the floor for a few minutes before getting up to clean himself up. As he looked in the bathroom mirror, he noticed it turned into a purple haze which started swirling around- all he could see and hear were the visions and sounds of war, of him shooting men, women, and children, a soldier that died in his arms, and his son gone forever. He felt the walls around him closing in, as if to crush him-suddenly, he let out a loud scream like one watching a horror movie. He had closed his eyes and opened them only to see a reflection in the mirror of a broken-hearted man who he hated. He took his fist and pounded the mirror to pieces- he felt no hurt from the glass cutting his knuckles, but felt excruciating pain from the scenes that played through his mind. He burst into tears releasing all the anguish that haunted and tormented him. Then, for the first time in his life, he prayed, "God, if you are real and I don't know if you even hear me, please help me." At that moment, something peaceful came over him as he made his way to his bed and fell asleep.

Chapter 15

"Oh crap!" my uncle shouted loudly as he woke up the next morning in dried up vomit. The stinking smell of liquor and appetizers permeated the air as he took off his clothes trying to remember what happened the previous night.

"I've got to clean this stuff up before Doug wakes up," my uncle said, not knowing that it was my father who vomited all over him and the couch.

My father was still sound asleep in his bedroom, as my uncle had finished cleaning the sofa and headed toward the shower. During his shower, my uncle had thought about taking my father fishing- it was something that they hadn't done in a long time and there was something about being on the waters that brought about a sense of serenity.

"Hey Doug, wake up, time to rise and shine," my uncle said as he knocked loudly on my father's bedroom door.

"Hold up man. My eyes are killing me. Feels like someone is pulling them from inside my head. What time is it anyway?" my father replied.

"It's morning time. Get on up. I got a surprise for you."

"Surprise?"

"Yeah. I'm taking you fishing. I got one of the locals in the village who will take us out on his boat and we can use his fishing equipment."

"Man, you're kidding me. You woke me up on an early Saturday morning to take me fishing- I don't feel like going fishing. Just let me lay in bed."

"Get your butt up and let's go soldier and that's an order," said my uncle as he glanced toward my father's bathroom and noticed the broken mirror and bloodstains on the floor.

"Man, what the hell happened there?" my uncle said pointing to my father's bathroom.

"Oh, I accidently hit the mirror thinking that I saw someone else," my father replied.

In actuality, my father did see another man in the mirror, a man who was consumed by demons of war and in danger of losing his soul. He would eventually find the Source that would give him a peaceful mind and forgive him for all his transgressions.

"You all right Doug?" my uncle asked.

My uncle's voice faded out in the background as my father's mind started wondering back through the years as if his life was flashing before his eyes. The voices of his past all spoke at once chanting in unison all the negativity he endured throughout his life:

"You'll never be anything. You're too dumb for school. You're worthless. You nappy-headed nigger, get your black behind out of my house."

That negativity would make him enlist in the U.S. Army at the age of 16.

"Earth calling Doug, Come in Doug," my uncle said again snapping his fingers in front of my father's face.

"Yeah, I'm OK. Just some cuts on the back of my hand," my father replied as he came back to reality.

"Shower yourself off and I'll clean this mess up."

My uncle had spotlessly cleaned up the broken pieces of glass and blood as my father had finished taking his shower.

"So, what's the deal with the fishing?" my father asked as he got dressed for the occasion.

"I thought it would do us some good to get on the water and have a peaceful interlude with nature and catch some fish. I've realize that we haven't been fishing since we left Ft. Bliss."

"I guess that would be kind of fun."

After my father had gotten dressed, they drove out toward the main gate into to village and met up with a local fisherman who escorted them to his boat. He had offered my father and uncle some hot tea as the boat sputtered out to sea. It had been a week since my father had returned from Korea and there was yet to be any lengthy conversations concerning Mitsuko and me. My uncle knew that my father still had a glimmer of hope in finding us, but it would take a miracle, which my father didn't believe miracles could happened- especially after praying for a young soldier who died in his arms.

"Doug," my uncle started off, "we've got to put Mitsuko and your son to rest. I don't think we'll ever going to find them."

There was a long silence between them as my father realized the words he didn't want to hear. He stared at the reflection of the sun's rays off the crystal clear blue waters looking for some type of solace in his spirit.

"He's my son," my father finally replied as he stayed in a continuous stare.

My uncle nodded his head in agreement as the two sat in silence for the rest of the afternoon looking over the sea and listening to the sounds of seagulls chirping overhead. Neither one cared about catching any fish.

The sun started to set as the boat made its way back to its harbor. After docking and a few friendly spoken exchanges, my uncle tipped the local twenty dollars, which he gladly accepted, for the local had made more than a day's wages. Shortly thereafter, my father and uncle hopped in their jeep and headed back to base. During the drive, my father finally broke his silence.

"I could go for some sake and fish since we didn't catch anything today."

"Sounds good to me," my uncle replied.

They stopped at their favorite place and Miss Tomiko welcomed them as they came inside. She had a big smile on her face, for this was the first time she had seen my father since his return from Korea.

"Me glad to see you- I think maybe you died in war," Miss Tomiko said with a chuckle. "I got special dish for you."

She brought out a couple plates of sushi rolls accompanied by 2 teacups of sake.

"That looks good," my uncle said as he sipped on his drink.

"Smells good too," my father said taking a deep inhaling smell of his sake and sushi with rice rolled in seaweed.

My father had taken his last sip of sake when he noticed tears running down my uncle's face.

"What's wrong with you Gill?"

"Shoot Doug, are we doing the right thing- you know, giving up on finding your son?"

"I can't question if it's the right thing, but there's nothing else we can do. You can't blame yourself. Like you said, it would take an army to help find them and we wouldn't even know where to begin. Hell, they could be in China or the Philippines."

My father attempted to pay Miss Tomiko, but she wouldn't accept his money- she said that their meal was on the house. He left the five-dollar bill on the table as my uncle and him left the restaurant and headed back to the base.

Chapter 16

EARLY THE NEXT MORNING, MY father had a staff meeting concerning his battalion's next deployment. He had found out that his platoon would be sent to fight in Vietnam, which was dreaded news to all those that had to go. They would all depart in 30 days after receiving some intensive ground training, afterwards being sent to Vietnam to help police the villages and fight guerilla forces. My father had hated hearing about Vietnam for there were many American causalities building up.

"That's some scary stuff," my father said to one of his platoon leaders.

"Yes sir it is," replied the platoon leader.

My father recalled that no one wanted to go to Vietnam. During May of 1965, President Lyndon B. Johnson would send the first U.S. Army battalion troops, which included my father's platoon. It would become the longest war in American history and the most unpopular American war of the twentieth century. It would result in nearly 60,000 American deaths and an estimated 2 million Vietnamese deaths. Even today, many Americans still ask whether the American effort in Vietnam was a sin, a blunder, a necessary war, or a noble cause, or an idealistic failed effort to protect the South Vietnamese from totalitarian government. My father's unit would be sent to the city of Hanoi, where one of the major battles of war took place. My father's assignment for his platoon would be to police the city and kill the enemy, known as the Viet Cong, by whatever means necessary.

"This war is a bunch of B.S.," shouted another platoon leader. "The damn French can't fight their own battles and now, we have to go and risk our lives for a war that we have nothing to do with- it's a bunch of propaganda B.S."

"I understand how you feel, but nonetheless, we have our orders from the top and we have to deploy," said one of the base commanders. "Hopefully, this deployment will be over quickly and all of you will be able to return home."

My father's mind had drifted from the deployment meeting as the rotation of the second hand on the wall clock put him in a hypnotic state. All he could think about was that he would never get to know his son; the first steps, the first day of school, the first bike ride, the childhood, teen, and adult years. Thirty days to do something before he would have to leave Okinawa without a clue as to the whereabouts of his son.

"God, please do something," said my father silently, this coming from a man who practiced Buddhism, which centralized around the ideology of re-incarnation.

"Sgt. Douglas, are you with us," said one of the base commanders noticing my father's continuous stare at the wall clock.

"Yes sir," my father replied. "Just thinking about Vietnam and my family sir."

"That's understandable considering that some of you will lose men including your own lives- that is why we need to pay strict attention to details and limit our casualties. Regardless of what opinions we have about Vietnam, we are here to protect and serve The United States of America and carry out the directives of the commander in chief. Godspeed gentlemen."

Back in the States, there were many protests of the Vietnam War including large demonstrations, flag burnings, student sit-ins at universities and colleges and the anti-draft rallies led by the "hippie" movement. These were accompanied by the Civil Rights Movement led by Martin Luther King, Jr., which protested the numerous drafting of black soldiers compared to white soldiers at the time. Vietnam would see the largest contingency of black men fighting and losing their lives for a country that failed to give them equal opportunity and treatment outside of the armed forces. However, a unity would developed, a special brotherhood, among the soldiers in all branches of service, regardless of color.

Chapter 17

"It's almost 4 a.m. guys. I say we all call it the night and continue this history lesson tomorrow evening," my father said to everyone as a big yawn came across his face. "I'm getting sleepy and I want to make sure that we're all well rested for our activities later in the day."

"Yep, I'm with you on that," my uncle replied.

Capt. Williams and Sgt. Johnson were also in agreement. My father had given them his keys to the car and gave directions back to the hotel.

"I would drive y'all, but I'm too tired. It's a straight shot there and back," my father said as he gave them hugs.

We all exchanged pleasantries and agreed to meet back around 5p.m. to continue the story.

"Well Freddie Jr., what do you think so far," my uncle asked, as my father had accompanied Sgt. Johnson and Capt. Williams out to the car.

"It's wow. I mean I would have never thought I was involved in all this. I can't remember Mitsuko or any of the guys that are here for my birthday. I'm still waiting on how I got here."

"We'll get into that later," my uncle said, as he gave me a two-fingered salute and headed for the guest room.

I had spent the next few hours reviewing the documents that my father gave me in attempt to piece together the story that was told throughout this night. There were pictures of Mitsuko and my father taken at various times during their courtship, pictures of my uncle and father together dressed in their respective uniforms, pictures of my mother and father in Okinawa, along with many pictures of me from kindergarten to elementary school. However, there was one picture that caught my attention- it was a picture of 11 men including my father, who was in the center holding a baby. There were names written underneath each person: Eddie Robinson (pilot),

Michael Nelson, Wallace Johnson, Earl Williams, Arthur Smith, Robert Roland, Steven Favors, Rodney Williams, James Gill, Fred Douglas, and Colonel Stephen Boyd. A written caption above the picture read, "True Unsung Heroes," which didn't make any sense for there was nothing to indicate any acts of heroism among these men. They were all smiles, some giving a thumbs-up, some giving the peace sign, and others looking at my father holding a baby.

"What is so special about this group of black men taking a picture with a white colonel and a white captain," I thought to myself. Through the years, I heard my father mentioned their names in phone conversations with my Uncle Gill referencing certain events of their service careers. Some were Army boxers that my father coached to several armed forces boxing championships as well as members of my father's platoon during the Korean conflict and Vietnam War. They were all loyal men who were dedicated to protecting the brotherhood of "black soldiers" under the leadership of my father- their struggles weren't against the enemies of war, but against their own country in recognizing them as equals and allowing them the opportunity to have a normal place in society. My father had once summed up the treatment of black soldiers in this way:

"We fight a war for our country protecting the lives and freedom of its citizens only to come back home to fight another war- racism. The government we protected fails to protect us when we were denied the rights and abilities to become equal citizens of this country. There were times when the U.S. Army uniform I wore didn't mean crap in my eyes- we were black men who were expendable in war and America could care less about how many of us needed help, allowing our families to suffer and eat crap. Those of us that died didn't receive proper burials or recognition- I heard a white officer once say, "replace a nigger with a nigger and eventually, we'll get rid of all niggers". Why should I fight for a country that didn't give a damn for us? There were times during the war when I was shooting at the enemy replacing the faces with the whites who called me "nigger" and threw rocks at me, spat in my face and made fun of the way I looked down to the clothes I wore. It made it easier for me to kill the enemy and become absorbed in a cycle of hatred that would be the driving rage in destroying whatever stood in my way. I stared death many times in the eyes of war, only to tell death to kiss my behind as I carried white soldiers many miles to safety, saving their lives, while they refused to carry us, leaving us to die. I lost my hope in the country I fought for, even losing hope in God for allowing these things to happen. I eventually became a Buddhist seeking peace and looking for sanity to my insanity."

It was twelve noon when I had awakened to the noises of barking dogs and a car driving by with its muffler dragging on the street. This would be the day that I would pick up my Torino and go on a triple date with my two best friends. I was even more excited about getting with my father, uncle and the rest of the gang to continue the story of my existence.

"You finally up," my father said, as he was cleaning fish that our next door neighbor had given from his early morning catch.

"Yeah, I'm up. Looks like we're having fish for lunch," I replied.

"Your mom said that she'll have to take a rain check on lunch with you- she went to the flea market with one of her friends and they'll be gone all day. After I get done, we'll go pick up the Torino."

"Sounds like a plan to me. Where's Uncle Gill?"

"He went with the others to MacDill to pick up some things. They should be back in a little while."

I had decided to take the time to ask my father questions about some of the documents that he had given me.

"The picture that has "true unsung heroes" written on it- what was that picture about?"

"Oh, you'll find out later. I want the others to give you their input on that picture," my father replied back.

"What's with the two white officers- the colonel and the captain?"

"That's Colonel Boyd and Capt. Williams. Colonel Boyd was our base commander during the time that picture was taken. He played a major role with the guys in the picture. You know Capt. Williams- you'll find out later what he did."

"Do you have any idea on where Mitsuko might be now?" I asked my father looking at Mitsuko's picture.

"She may be back in Okinawa. The only way to find out for sure would be to check with the Japanese Government Registry of Records. They may have some information. Why do you want to know?"

"Well, in case I may want to search for her one day just to see what she look like and if she would know me."

"I don't know if that would be such a good idea. I mean, there's a lot more you haven't heard yet about Mitsuko. Besides, as far as I'm concern, Yoshiko is your mother."

"She's the only mother I know. I just wanted to see if Mitsuko was still alive and get a chance to see the woman that birthed me. By no means can she ever take my mother's place."

My father and I had talked for a while longer- he was careful not to divulge any information until later when the others arrived. He kept reassuring me that all my questions would be answered in due time. With that said, I was ready to pick up my car.

Chapter 18

"OH MAN, THAT'S A BAD car!" I shouted to my father. "Wait till my buddies see me in this."

I sat in the car listening to "Sara Smile" by Hall and Oates, as I sung in unison with the song being played on the radio. My father had a new speaker system installed in the car and the music was like a live concert being performed.

"Ok son, you're all set to ride," my father said. "Be careful and pay attention to others around you."

"I gotcha," I replied back, jamming to Wild Cherry's "Play That Funky Music White Boy" blasting through the speakers, as I drove down the street looking to see who was paying attention to me.

I could see the reflection of my red Torino in the glass window of a storefront office- I thought I was cool looking at my reflection and giving myself a thumbs- up. I saw a girl looking at me, as I couldn't resist the urge to show off a little by revving my V-8 engine and screeching my tires on the take-off on the green light. I hadn't noticed that my father was a car behind me and saw what I was doing- I would hear about it later at home.

"All right Starsky and Hutch," my uncle said as I pulled up into the driveway at home. "That's a nice ride."

"Thanks. I love this car," as I motioned for my uncle to get in on the passenger side.

"This sucker is fast too. I think I like this better than that mustang I was hoping to get."

I drove my uncle around the block showing him all the "belts and whistles" of the car. My uncle shook his head in amazement as he gave me a joyous smile; somehow I had sense that his amazement was not at my young expertise as a driver, but at the young man that was sitting beside him driving. All he kept saying was, "miracles."

The phone was ringing as I entered the house to change for my upcoming date with my friends.

"Hey Fred, bad news- Miguel and I won't be able to keep our date this evening. We forgot that we had promise to take our little brothers to Busch Gardens for the day and my mom won't let me break my promise," Ivan said as he was trying to conjure up excuses to break his promise.

"No sweat. We can do it tomorrow. I'll just called the girls and let them know. Cool?" I replied.

"Cool, that's a bet. I'll call you tomorrow."

I was kind of glad that our date was cancelled because I wanted to stay home and continue the conversations with my father, uncle and their friends. I was anxious to find out about where all these guys came from and why they were considered "unsung heroes" as well as their roles in my life. I couldn't quite figure out the connection with them, especially with Capt. Williams, who acted more "black" than his white skin suggested. He had more "ties" with my Uncle Gill than with my father, but my father always considered him a good friend and a brother. My uncle had said this about Capt. Earl Williams:

"Earl pushed me to become one the few black captains of the Air Force risking his own career by refusing to obey a superior officer to remove me from consideration of being promoted. He told the superior officer that if I was removed from consideration, he would have him reported to The Pentagon brass for racism and "conduct unbecoming of an officer." Needless to say, it helped that Earl was related to a top General at The Pentagon who could make life uncomfortable for any officer who was a racist. I believe that Earl had something to do with all of us being stationed together for most of our service careers. Earl hung around more black people that he started picking up some of the dialect and slang that we were using. Heck, he even married a black woman."

The honking of a loud horn caught my attention as I looked outside the window and saw my father with the others getting out of the car carrying bags of chips, soda, and beer. There was still plenty of leftover ribs and chicken from the day before to eat; this would be another festive gathering of "old men" who would swap more stories and engage me in the story of my life.

Chapter 19

WE WERE ALL SITTING IN the patio area of the backyard listening to the sounds of Marvin Gaye; the cold cans of Colt 45 lined the table as my father, uncle and the others were exchanging family stories. I could hear from the kitchen Sgt. Johnson talking about his 18-year-old daughter saying how great she had been in school and she had a bright future- he hinted to my father that it would be nice if I met her.

"That could be a possibility," my father said. "They're both the same age. The only problem is the distance."

"Hey, I got a daughter that's a couple of years older," said Capt. Williams. "And she's a knockout."

"Well, we know she didn't get her looks from you," my uncle replied, grinning and pointing at Capt. Williams. "Anyway, I've seen your daughter and she's too tall for Freddie Jr. But, she is beautiful."

I came outside with an aluminum pan full of ribs and chicken for everyone to eat and eat we did.

"You know Earl got some black in him- that's how you eat a rib, right down to the bone," my uncle said laughing.

After we all ate, my uncle asked if everyone was already to commence with their stories of Okinawa and me.

"Yeah, let's do this because I'm anxious myself to find out what led up to our part," said Sgt. Johnson. "I believe we left off after finding out about going to Vietnam and how everyone was protesting about the war and stuff."

My father and uncle were gathering their thoughts trying to remember details of what took place during this time frame. My father would lead off, as the others would add to the conversations about my life drifting back to late March of 1965:

The ringing of the phone woke my father as he peeked at the clock. "Who in the hell would be calling me at 4 a.m." he said to himself.

"Hello, Hello, Doug, wake up, it's Gill"

"Gill, what the hell is going on- you know what time it is?"

"Doug, get dressed quickly and I'll be by to pick you up in 10 minutes."

"10 minutes? What's going on Gill," my father said with a look of sleepy confusion.

"We may have a break on Mitsuko and Freddie Jr." my uncle replied in hurried excitement.

My father was in shock and disbelief as he put on his uniform pants and t-shirt, brushed his teeth, combed his hair and waited for my uncle outside. It had been nearly 2 years since my father last saw me- he wondered if it could be true that I was still around. My father had started to come to terms with reality that he would never see me again- now, the news possibly seeing me sparked a little hope in his heart.

My uncle had picked up my father within the 10 minutes he had said and they headed over to Air Recon Support Center.

"I got a call around 3 a.m. this morning from a friend of mine, Capt. Williams, saying that one of his operatives may have information on the location where Mitsuko and Freddie Jr. may be at."

"Are you sure Gill?" my father replied. "I mean this would be a miracle if it's true."

"We'll find out in a few," my uncle said as they pulled up to the support center.

"Sgt. Douglas and Sgt. Gill reporting as ordered sir!" said my uncle and father as they saluted Colonel Boyd, not expecting him to be present.

"At ease gentlemen and we can cut the formality stuff," replied Colonel Boyd. "Doug, Gill, I like you to meet Capt. Earl Williams from Kadena- Gill, I believe you and Earl are already acquainted with each other."

"Yes sir," my uncle replied as he gave Capt. Williams a short hugging handshake.

Capt. Williams had been an advocate of my uncle in trying to get him in the officer's selection program. They went through basic training together and even though both of them were opposite in race, an immediate friendship was formed that would last a lifetime to come. My uncle was more than qualified to become an officer, but because of his race, he was overlooked for lesser- qualified white men. However, Capt. Williams would eventually present his case for my uncle and have him placed in Officer's Candidate School with eventual promotion to Captain.

After the exchanging of handshakes and greetings, Colonel Boyd confirmed what my uncle told my father.

"Capt. Williams may have information concerning your son, Doug-This is strictly off the record and stays in this room. We can all get our butts fried for this."

"Yes sir," both my father and uncle replied.

My father was very fond of Colonel Stephen Boyd as an officer and a personal friend. Colonel Boyd had befriended my father in having him selected to coach the Army boxing team, which under my father, won many boxing championships. Colonel Boyd believed that my father was a superb boxer and should've become a professional boxer, but my father didn't want to deal with race issues. Colonel Boyd was convinced that my father could have beaten another great boxer by the name of Cassius Clay, better known as Muhammad Ali- even my uncle had concurred that my father was a great boxer. Instead, my father became a great boxing coach and even coached Colonel Boyd in several fights, winning them all.

"Capt. Williams will go over the information that his operatives gave him," Colonel Boyd said, as he gestured Capt. Williams to take over the conversation.

'Call me Earl since this is informal and behind closed doors. As Colonel Boyd mentioned, we all can get in huge trouble over this," Capt. Williams said as he unrolled a map of Japan that was highlighted with markings.

Capt. Williams gave this account of what led to the highlighted map:

"I had received a phone call from one of my Japanese operatives who came in contact with a man who had recognized Mitsuko and the baby from a picture that had been circulating around Sendai. My operative paid a handsome price for the information and relayed it to me at Kadena. After studying the information, I deployed an Air Recon team, which I accompanied, to perform secret flight surveillance over Sendai. This was dangerous for us since the U.S. agreed not to perform any type of surveillance without the consent of the Japanese government. Anyway, I had to take a chance and verify the information I had was correct. Gill had told me about what happened with Mitsuko and the baby and I knew that if I could help in anyway, I would do whatever I can to help. After going on a couple of missions, which I coded as ground rescue training, my team took enough photos as we were able to get a few men on the ground to take pictures of a fenced compound, which I believe could be where Mitsuko and the baby are held. This area is highlighted on the aerial map around Sendai."

Everyone took a moment to study the pictures that were being passed around along with the highlighted markings on the map.

"Any idea who controls this camp?" asked Colonel Boyd.

"We're not 100 percent sure, but the reports we have show that it may belong to a Japanese rebel black market group known as the Yakamoto," replied Capt. Williams. "The Yakamoto are an organized group that sold weapons, drugs, and "war" babies to anyone that was willing to pay their price. We believe that your wife, Mitsuko, is a part of this organization and had a baby by you for this purpose."

My father couldn't believe what he was hearing as he blurted out, "you got to be joking me."

'Think about it Doug- did she ever reveal anything to you about her family, her background, did you ever meet any of her peoples?" asked Capt. Williams.

My father replayed scenes of Mitsuko and him during their conversations during their courtship and couldn't recall any information she revealed about her family, friends, or where she came from. The only thing she say that both her parents had died and that she had some family members on the mainland of Japan, which she didn't keep in contact.

"You're right Earl," my father said.

"Damn Doug, I told you there was something about her from the get-go," my uncle added.

Capt. Williams had described the compound, which the rebels occupied and how they ran their operations.

"Our Intel reports that they have snipers within a mile area of their compound," he said as he pointed to certain markings on the map. "They may also have booby traps set up also."

Capt. Williams showed the blueprints of the compound explaining what it would take to break through the compound.

"It's going to take a small army to get inside and that's where the problem lies," Capt. Williams said as he and the others looked at Colonel Boyd.

Colonel Boyd knew what everyone was thinking and immediately explained that the Army couldn't have any participation or knowledge of what was being discussed.

"I cannot authorize any involvement in this. This could lead to a major thrift with the Japanese government and that's something we don't need. I couldn't even get clearance to send men to do this. Then, we're not even sure if Mitsuko and Doug's son are inside that compound."

"But, they could be there- how am I supposed to get my son?" my father said, looking at Colonel Boyd.

"Doug, I empathize with your situation, and even if I wanted to allow support, the Army along with the U.S. Government would have all of our butts buried. Hell, this information we have now is enough to cause us all to be court-martialed. Sorry Doug, but there's nothing I can do. My hands are tied."

"I understand your position sir, but that doesn't stop me from going in alone and get my son," my father replied.

"Doug, you're crazy, you'll never make it alive. These rebels have a small army of their own. You'll never make it alone," said Capt. Williams.

"I don't care. If there's a chance that my son could be there, I've got to try. I could never live with myself knowing that I didn't go after my son when I had the chance."

The room filled with silence for a moment as my father had made up his mind that he was coming after his son no matter what anyone said.

"Just the thought of not trying is worse than facing death in battle," my father said as he stood and looked at everyone. "I appreciate everyone's input, but you have to understand my position. This is my son we're talking about. I will do this alone."

"Doug, I can't allow you to do this. If I have to keep you in protective custody until your unit leaves for deployment, I will," said Colonel Boyd. "I can't allow you to risk your life for an assumption. You have a unit to lead and your men need you to lead them," replied Colonel Boyd.

"Sir, with all due respect, if you knew your only son was still alive and you had the opportunity to at least see for yourself, could you turn your back on him?" my father asked Colonel Boyd.

"Doug, I understand, but you're asking me not only allow you to risk your life, but also the careers of the men in this room. If something were to happen to you, the Army would point their finger at me, and Capt. Williams, for illegally obtaining this information. I'm sorry Doug, but I have to look at the big picture."

There was again another silence in the room. Then a voice that was silent finally spoke.

"Sir, can I speak to you in private," my uncle said to Colonel Boyd.

Colonel Boyd had instructed everyone not to discuss this matter and to get rid of all documents as he motioned for my uncle to meet him in the adjoining room. My father sat in his chair, motionless, as his mind was already planning on how he could get to me. Capt. Williams gathered the maps and pictures as he asked my father if he was going to be ok. My father didn't say a word and didn't have to; Capt. Williams said that the expression and tears from my father's face said it all.

Chapter 20

A COUPLE OF DAYS HAD passed since my father's meeting with Colonel Boyd and Captain Williams. He had stayed in his apartment the entire time pondering himself on whether he should disobey orders and come after me and suffer the consequences, even if it meant death, or should he forget about finding me just as Colonel Boyd said, giving the reasons. My father gave this account of this time:

"I couldn't get any sleep the past couple of nights since finding out the possibility of seeing my son existed. I understood Colonel Boyd's position on my situation and he had to protect the interest of the U.S. Army and the U.S. Government. Any undisclosed involvement with the Japanese would cause serious damage to U.S. - Japanese relations at this critical time. But, I could do it alone without anyone knowing or could I? Capt. Williams was right- it would take a small army to help rescue my son. I was trying desperately to convince myself that it was the right thing to forget about my son, but my inner conscious wouldn't let me rest. There was something that could be done. I was at the end of my rope- I asked God to intervene despite my belief in Buddha. If anything was going to be done, it had to be done soon- there was a little over 3 weeks until I would leave Okinawa. Oh God, please do something."

It was at my father's last request of God when a loud knock at the door disrupted his thoughts. It was my Uncle Gill shouting for my father to open the door.

"Hey Doug, open the door, we have to report to Colonel Boyd's office right away."

"Hold your horses man, I'm coming," my father replied, as he unlocked the door. "What's the entire hurrying Gill?"

"No time to talk, we have to go," my uncle said pulling my father by his arm. "No time to explain."

My uncle drove quickly to Colonel Boyd's office not paying attention to any stop signs or stoplights, but being careful to avoid possible accidents. My father continuously questioned my uncle only to receive a response of "you'll see when we get there."

My father and uncle entered Colonel Boyd's office as Capt. Williams ran up behind them. Capt. Williams and my uncle exchanged nodding glances as Colonel Boyd stood up to greet them.

"Thanks for coming on such short notice. Doug, I guess you're wondering what's going on?" said Colonel Williams.

Indeed, my father had been wondering what was going on and why Capt. Williams and my uncle seemed to know what was about to unfold. My father had thought maybe his unit was being deployed earlier than expected or he was being sent to another unit- a thousand thoughts raced through his mind as he tried to maintained focus on Colonel Boyd.

"Yes sir, I am puzzled. Is my unit being deployed early?" replied my father.

"Oh, nothing like that Doug. Gill, won't you do the honors and tell Doug what we discussed since it was your idea. Earl, you can help fill in the gaps."

"Doug, we may have the opportunity to go after Freddie Jr. The Colonel has agreed to allow one mission, but there are stipulations, which I will cover," said my uncle.

"Are you serious? I mean are we really going to get my son?" said my father.

"Just listen Doug," replied Colonel Boyd.

My uncle went on to explain that there were 4 search and rescue-training missions headed for the southern mountain country of Japan, which was approved by the Japanese Government.

"Let's say that if one of these missions accidently went off course and headed for Sendai and landed near the outskirts of the Yakamoto compound. And let's say if there happened to be 6 men on the training team, which included you Doug, that would enter the compound and find Freddie Jr. and bring him back. Sounds good right? Easier said than done.

We could possibly have a bloody fight on our hands with the Yakamoto snipers and the rest of their gunmen."

"You're right Gill, easier said than done. But, I thought the Colonel said that the Army couldn't be involved?" asked my father.

"You're right Doug, but if we do this, this mission never existed- no records, no paper trail, nobody knows anything. If this gets out, I'll have everyone here court-martialed and dishonorably discharged," replied Colonel Boyd.

My father had a puzzled look as he asked why the Colonel had a change in heart and involve himself in this matter.

"Gill and I spoke after my meeting with you and made me realize that I owe you- you're a good man Doug and a great soldier. I too, had a son and lost him at war- I know how it feels to lose a son. But, as I said, the Army, the U.S. Government, and the Japanese Government have no knowledge and must not know what you're all about to do should we decide to go through with these plans. The stipulation that comes is that if this plan gets leaked out or if you're caught, I'm excluded from this and I will have to follow Army regulations and have you and all those involve brought before high command. Do I make myself clear?"

"Yes sir. The Colonel doesn't know a thing. But, we won't get caught," replied my father with Capt. Williams and my uncle nodding in agreement.

"OK, with that said, I will do what I can to help. Earl, take over from here," said Colonel Boyd.

"I have everything we'll need to accomplish this mission except for the eight men that will accompany us on this mission. Doug, this has strictly got to be voluntary with the consequences known. Gill and I will come with you so you only need six men. Also, I got two pilots that will fly the mission. Any suggestions on the six?" said Capt. Williams.

"Yeah, I got six I know will volunteer with no questions asked," my father replied, as he grabbed a pen and started writing the names of six men.

The names my father wrote were not only members of my father's platoon, but also members of his boxing team. These men were very loyal to him and would be willing to risk their lives for him. All would volunteer immediately without hesitation even after hearing the consequences of being caught or captured.

These were the men that volunteered:

Wallace Johnson, Rodney Williams, Steven Favors, Arthur Smith, Robert Roland, and Michael Nelson.

Sergeant Wallace Johnson gave this account of the men that volunteered:

"Sergeant Douglas called me to attend a special meeting at battalion headquarters. I had no idea or clue to why he was calling this meeting- I thought perhaps it had something to do with me getting a little rowdy in one of the village bars, which I accidently grabbed one of the waitresses and was almost engaged in a fight. If Sarge had found out, I was about to get my butt handed to me. Sergeant Douglas was firm, but fair, and all the men under his command were crazy about him- he stood up for what was right and didn't take crap off anybody, whether you were a superior officer or not. By us being an all black platoon, we were always the last on the list to get what we needed. Sergeant Douglas stood up for us when we were treated wrong because of our color; there's a difference in being treated as soldiers in the Army versus being treated as "niggers" in a white man's army. All the young black men, including myself, looked up to Sergeant Douglas as a role model and a father figure. He even took some of us under his wing and molded us into championship boxers for the Army boxing team. We might not have been 100 percent loyal to the Army, but we would give our souls for Sergeant Douglas- he was that kind of leader as well as a man who stood his ground when wrongdoing was done toward us. He earned the respect of Colonel Boyd and most the high command as he always took responsibility for the actions of his men, whether we were right or wrong. If you were wrong, you best believe your butt was grass behind closed doors. He never fussed at us in front of anyone- he believed in always presenting a strong united unit in front of all the white superior officers. When I had arrived at battalion headquarters, I was relieved to see some of my fellow soldiers standing around waiting for an explanation as to why we were all called. Sergeant Douglas, Sergeant Gill, and Captain Williams came out the office and motioned for all of us to sit down. Sergeant Douglas thanked us for coming and quickly explained the situation surrounding the possible rescue of his son and that this was strictly a volunteer mission due to the consequences involved. I believe the trio was shocked when all the men present volunteered before we were even asked. This was something we could do for our sergeant and not the Army."

Chapter 21

COLONEL BOYD HAD MADE IT possible for my father, uncle, and all the men involved with the rescue mission to be excused from their daily duties to meet and train for this special mission. Capt. Williams would head up the planning in discussing every detail to ensure no mistakes were made. The Colonel again had stressed that there was no room for error and that any detection of their involvement would be devastating for all the men involved. They all understood that the Colonel would deny any authorization or knowledge of what was going on. These were trusted loyal men and they were ready to accept any consequences if they were exposed- they understood their roles and the Colonel was to be protected at all costs. Colonel Boyd had arranged for one of the empty aircraft hangers to serve as a training facility for the special mission and provided everything that was needed for the men involved. As Colonel Boyd stated, "Gentlemen, we will be perfect in every aspect of this mission- there is absolutely no room for error. I will provide everything within my authority to give you what you need."

Capt. Williams had planned that it would take about 5 to 7 days to nail down all the details to perfection and memory. There would be 20 hour days of going over every detail until each man knew his assignment without thought. This is Capt. Williams' account of this time period:

"With the help of Colonel Boyd, I used the surveillance pictures to re-enact the rebel compound inside the empty aircraft hangar to help give us a realistic view of what we would be facing. I even had a helicopter placed 3 miles from the hangar that would be the duplication of where the copter would be during the live mission. I spent almost 36 hours going over every detail of recon information that I gathered during the so-called search and rescue training missions. I had sniper towers built around the makeshift compound along with the housing units. It was my responsibility to make sure these men could perform their tasks to perfection and within the time allotted. Time would be a major factor since we only had 55 minutes to get in and out before the Japanese recon planes flew over- a minute late and we would be spotted by them- this would cause serious friction with the Japanese Government in what was already a delicate relationship and land us in a heap of trouble with our own government. The key would be not to engage the enemy in a gun battle, which could become a bloody show, especially us being outnumbered 3 to 1. It was no coincidence that the men chosen were also master marksmen- their skills would be tested and pushed to the limit."

"Okay men, welcome to operation "baby rescue" day 1. All of you have been initially brief by Sgt. Gill on the purpose of this mission and as volunteers, you all understand the consequences if we failed to execute the plan to perfection. It is my duty to make sure that all of you will be perfect in every aspect of this mission. Any questions?" asked Capt. Williams.

"What is the timeframe before we execute this mission?" asked one of the men.

"The goal is 5 days from today," replied Capt. Williams. "Any more questions?"

After a couple of minutes of thoughtful silence, Capt. Williams instructed everyone to get ready to go to work. He had everyone gather around the conference table as blueprints, maps and photos were laid out for each of the men. The maps provided detail information on the landing mark of their helicopter to the rebel's sniper towers. The pictures provided detail structures of the sniper towers, the front entrance, the housing units, and the possible occupants of those housing units. The blueprints gave close to exact replica of the rebel's compound inside the aircraft hangar.

"We have exactly 55 minutes from landing to get the baby and be back in the air before Japanese Recon flies over. Step one is that all seven of you have to make it from the copter to the sniper towers in 15 minutes. I have positioned the copter 3 miles from our landing pad to the sniper towers you see here inside this hangar. All of you will run from the copter to this hangar in 15 minutes or less- that's the same 3 miles that you'll run in live action, however, keep in mind that you will be running through wooded areas," said Capt. Williams, as he motioned everyone toward the

Chinook helicopter. "Everyone should be in full gear including backpacks and weapons. I will time all of you as a group and the last man to reach the hangar will stop the time. Gentlemen, we will repeat this exercise until we are within the 15 minute window. Is everyone clear?"

"Yes sir!" everyone replied in unison.

"Doug, you will lead your men. Gill, you will start the time on Doug and I will stop the time on the last man at the hangar."

My uncle had called everyone in a huddle to give words of encouragement and remind everyone the importance of completing this exercise on time. In fact, he told everyone that they should be able to complete the exercise in 13 minutes since they're running a straight line without any obstacles. They all agreed to the 13 minute mark as Capt. Williams called for everyone to get ready. My father had instructed everyone to line up in front of the helicopter as he shouted, "the last person to cross the finish line is a rotten egg!" There was a chuckle among the men as my uncle shouted for everyone to get ready.

"On the whistle," said my uncle as he placed the whistle in his mouth. He radioed Capt. Williams to report that the men were ready to go. Capt. Williams radioed back as my uncle blew his whistle; it was like a thundering herd of horses taking off from the landing pad toward the hangar.

My uncle gave this account of this training exercise:

"I knew that Capt. Williams told them 15 minutes was the target, but I knew that they needed to complete the run in 13 minutes or less to make up for the wooded jungle conditions, which they would be placed. I knew that this would push the limit for all men, but I knew that their adrenaline would push them- this was a very competitive group and took the challenge of doing something near impossible as a threat to their manhood. Besides, they had to prove to Doug that there were no limits on whatever they had to do- they were going to be perfect. 'Perficio' became their motto, which means 'perfect till the end.' I was impressed with the brotherhood and teamwork exemplified by these men without regards to their own being, but showing concern for the other in pushing each other to be 'perficio' at all costs. The U.S. Army molded these men to become war machines, but it was Doug that molded these young black soldiers into men of character and honor. Some of these men would later become members of an elite force known as the U.S. Army Rangers."

"Fifteen minutes, forty seconds," shouted Capt. Williams, as the last man had cross the line at the hangar.

'Damn!" said one of the men in response to the time. They didn't place blame on the last man, but on themselves as a whole. They all headed back toward the helicopter in disappointed silence- nothing had to be said for they all knew what needed to be done and Capt. Williams along with my uncle, kept silent. My father looked at his men as they lined up again for another run admiring the determination in their eyes. My father gave this account of what happened:

"After we all completed the first run and heard the time called out to us by Capt. Williams, I was disappointed- I just knew we ran a great time. I could see the men were also disappointed, but they did something I thought they would never do- they all looked at each other as each individual took the blame for not being 'perficio' and giving commitments to one another to do better. Usually, they would yell at the one who was the weakest link and intimidate him to do better. There is a certain look that a soldier gave when you knew that nothing else needed to be said –they knew what had to be done and you could bet all the tea in China that they were going to do it. I knew that nothing was going to stop them except death and even then, death would have to bring something strong."

Once again, my uncle blew the starting whistle as all seven men took off running. My uncle said that he could notice more energy and concentration in their running as if they were chasing something. At one point, my uncle even said that all seven men were step for step, left-right, left-right, sounding like drums in a symphony orchestra.

"Thirteen minutes, thirty-three seconds," shouted Capt. Williams, as the last man cross the line. "Great job!"

Even though they had all exceeded the time set by Capt. Williams, there was still a look of disappointment in their eyes.

"Hey, you guys more than exceeded the time- why the disappointed faces?" asked Capt. Williams.

"We didn't make it less than thirteen minutes," replied my father.

Capt. Williams didn't understand why the men were upset about running a great time, especially a time that would set a record on a regular three-mile obstacle course. Before Capt. Williams could ask any more questions, the group of seven headed back toward starting point as my father shouted back to reset the time for another run.

"You've got to be kidding," said Capt. Williams to himself. He radioed my uncle to let him know that the group would be attempting another run. He told my uncle he didn't know why, but knew that it was important for them to break the thirteen-minute mark, which was very rare for a three-mile full gear run. My uncle replied back that by running the course in thirteen minutes, it would ensure a fifteen minute run through the wooded jungle areas leading to the rebel compound.

My uncle blew the whistle as the group of seven again ran liked drums beating in an orchestra, this time the beat was a little faster.

As the last man crossed the line, Capt. Williams stopped the timer and dropped his jaw. He had never seen such a time and knew that no one would ever believe such a time was achieved. My father was standing in a corner by himself trying to catch his breath as the other six men gathered around Capt. Williams looking at his stopwatch. As each man left the hangar, they passed by my father pointing a finger at him as they exited. They were all silent, except for this time, there were no disappointed faces. Capt. Williams came up to my father, still looking in awed and put the stopwatch in my father's hand. My father looked at the stopwatch and a smile cracked his face. Twelve minutes, forty-three seconds. "Perficio."

Chapter 22

AFTER A GOOD NIGHT'S REST, the group of seven, my uncle and Capt. Williams, assembled at the hangar for day 2 of "Operation Baby-Rescue".

"Ok gentlemen, today, we will concentrate on eliminating the enemy snipers from the towers," said Capt. Williams, as he continued explaining the objectives for the day. "The pictures you have show the proximity of the towers in relation to where the copter will land. After yesterday's performance, I have no doubt that you will be able to cover the three mile run through these wooded areas in less than fifteen minutes. As you can see on your pictorial map, the sniper towers are circled and approximately one hundred yards from the towers is another circle marked in red. This red circle is where you will shoot the men in the sniper towers. Your marksman skill will be tested as you will have only one shot, a hundred yards away."

"That's no problem," said one of the men.

"It shouldn't be for you guys. Oh, by the way, the lights in the hangar will be turned off- you will have to find your target and shoot him in total darkness."

"You got to be kidding. How do you expect us to see in the dark," replied one of the men.

"Remember gentlemen, it will be pitch dark when we land and you will have no lighting to go by for the exception of these," said Capt. Williams as he opened a box which contained infrared goggles made for night vision.

"These gentlemen are the newest technology that will aid in finding the enemy in the dark. I believe that Sgt. Douglas is the only one that has any experience using infrared vision goggles. The rest of you will train on using them tonight to take out your target."

"Did you say tonight, sir?" asked one of the men.

"Yes, tonight. We will meet at the landing pad at 22 hundred hours. Be in full gear with your goggles on. The main objective is that we're simulating what it will be under real conditions."

Capt. Williams went on to explain the intricacies of using the infrared goggles and the agenda for the overnight training. He explained while wearing the infrared goggles, they will run from the landing pad to the entrance of the hangar and all will have one shot at the fake "dummies" staged in the towers. Special training ammo will be used to splatter dye on contact to indicate if the "dummies" were hit. Each weapon will only be loaded with one bullet to give the men only one shot at eliminating their target. Since there were six targets, my father being the seventh man, would be the backup if one of the targets wasn't taken out on the first shooting.

"All right men, be well rested for tonight. We will do these exercises until we are 'perficio' three consecutive times," said Capt. Williams as he dismissed all the men.

My father had stayed behind to study the pictures of the housing units inside the compound. He knew that no mistakes could be made once they were inside and his search would be limited to time- he would have only one chance to find the right baby and bring everyone back before Japanese recon planes would fly over. The "what if" syndrome plagued his mind as he tried to concentrate on the surveillance pictures showing where the babies and women were kept.

"What if I can't find him? What if we mess up? What if we run out of time? What if we get shot? What if we get spotted?" my father thought to himself.

My father had mulled over the idea of just calling off the mission convincing himself that it probably would be a wasted effort, but his conscious wouldn't allow him to speak of quitting. Besides, he had a group of men that wouldn't allow him to quit.

A C130 plane thundered overhead as Capt. Williams, my uncle and the group of seven were all meeting at the landing pad preparing for the first run of the night's exercise. Their objective was to run from the landing pad to the hangar entrance within thirteen minutes and then with one shot, eliminate the "dummy" target. Capt. Williams had their Colt Commando rifles loaded with color-coded bullets, which upon contact with a target would eject a dye colored paint. A game of the future called "paintball" would evolve from these Army exercises and generate huge profits for game makers.

"Same thing as yesterday gentlemen with the exception of the infrared goggles. I will not time the first run since this is your first time wearing these goggles. You will have to learn to adjust to the night vision while maintaining the plan of events in your mind. It's not as easy as it looks," said Capt. Williams as he instructed the men to put their goggles on.

Oh man, this thing is wild," said one of the men looking through his infrared goggles. "Everything is bright green."

After taking several minutes for each man to focus their vision through the infrared goggles, Capt. Williams had instructed everyone to line up at the landing pad for the first run.

This is Sgt. Williams's account of this first run:

"It was crazy looking through those infrared goggles. We were all tripping over our own feet let alone over each other. For most of us, this was our first experience wearing infrared goggles and I felt real uncomfortable wearing them. Our first run was disastrous as it took twenty minutes to run the course and all of us missed shooting our targets. There was paint splattered on the walls, ceiling and the hangar door from our initial shots- we completely missed the "dummy" targets. Even Sgt. Douglas had problems hitting the targets, but at least, his shots hit the sniper towers. Man, it was crazy. It was the first time I felt embarrassed and helpless not being able to execute what seemed like a simple task. But the good news was that we eventually became used to the infrared goggles as we were able to complete the run in the allotted time and take out our target with one shot. It took us all night till sunrise the next morning- each man had refused to quit until the exercise was "perficio" over and over again. We all were totally exhausted, but we knew what was at stake and we couldn't let Sgt. Douglas down."

The sun was rising as Capt. Williams directed everyone to rest and meet back up at 10 pm in full gear and ready to run. My uncle gave everyone a high-five for their performance and effort in staying up all night. My father gave a silent nod of approval toward my uncle as he left the hangar and headed home. The "what if" doubts were slowly disappearing from my father's mind and being replaced with visions of a father and his son.

The Heart of a Father

The heart speaks well of a man
His tears and sweat are priceless
Who is a father to his children
And a husband of honor to his wife
He sacrifices for them everyday

Patience is his greatest asset
Wisdom and knowledge guides his feet
He bears the burden while being joyful
Becoming a shield from the storms of life
His hugs brings protection and peace

He gives freely to those in need
Even the shirt off his back he would offer
Never to expect anything in return
Just to be a blessing is his reward
His kindness and gentleness is his crown

A man will run from the fires of life
But a father will put the fires out
No recognition does he desire
Just the satisfaction from his soul
Knowing that he made a difference

A man can sow many seeds
But a father knows his children
He nurtures them like a tender plant
Watching them grow and flourish
Cherishing each moment with them

The world would be a better place
If we had more fathers than men
A man without love will perish
But a father's love will last forever
For this is the true heart of a father.

Chapter 23

I T WAS LATE AFTERNOON AS the sound of thunderous planes caught everyone's attention- all eyes were focused on the triangular formation of planes new to the air base.

"Oh man, who are those guys," asked my father.

"They're a new unit setting up called Operation OXCART performing on a mission known as 'Black Shield'. They have been assigned by top brass to patrol Communist China. That's all I've been told," replied Capt. Williams, as he was preparing the men for day three of their own mission training. "Great job getting through the first two days without any major problems. This evening, we will review the recon photos and blueprints of the rebel compound."

"Good," said one of the men. "No running involved."

After a brief chuckle by Capt. Williams, he went on to explain the recon information to the group of seven and my uncle.

"Air Recon Support photos show that there are eight housing units inside the compound," Capt. Williams said as he pointed to the houses circled in red on the enlarged photo attached to the bulletin board. "The three housing units on the left are where the men are living and the three on the right are the women's and children's units. The two in the back are bathrooms. Upon taking out the sniper towers, you will have five minutes to search each unit. My recommendation is that you pair up in two's with the exception of Doug and hit the three units where the men will be sleeping. Your job will be to execute them in their sleep as to leave no clues or identification of who we are. I know it sounds harsh, but this is considered an act of war- remember, your lives are at stake and they will shoot to kill you- the last thing we want is to engage all of them in a mini-battle. If we leave any alive that can identify us, our butts will be in a boatload of trouble with two governments- ours and the Japanese. Doug, after your men have eliminated their housing units, they will regroup with you at the first housing unit where the women and children are sleeping. Four men will guard the outside while the other two will accompany you inside each unit where you will have five minutes to search for your son. Anything more than five minutes will put this operation in jeopardy- we have to be completed and back in the air within fifty-five minutes. Gill will keep you advised of the time through radio communication. Doug, I know it's been about a year and a half, but I need you to make sure you can identify your son for there will be a few babies present. You will not have time to guess."

Capt. Williams looked sternly at my father and reiterated that he must be able to identify his son quickly for time would be of great essence.

"I know my son," replied my father in a convincible tone. "If he is there, I will find him."

"I know you will Doug," said Capt. Williams. "And one more thing, at any time this mission seems unsuccessful to the point of us being identified, we will abort and retreat back to copter and leave- I know I sound like a broken record, but we cannot risk our identification by the Japanese. Does everyone understand- this is a direct order if you hear 'abort mission' over the radio."

"Yes sir," all replied.

Capt. Williams had instructed everyone to spend the rest of the evening studying their folders, which contained the photos, blueprints, and plans that he had outlined to them. They were to submit everything to memory, for the next two days would be timing exercises covering the beginning and ending of the entire mission to under fifty-five minutes. The next two nights would stretch the entire group to their limits physically and emotionally.

Capt. Williams had wanted to meet with both my father and uncle after the evening exercises to discuss the progress of the training and put a timeline on the actual mission. My father had suggested meeting at Miss Tomiko's for a late dinner- he had been craving her yakisoba and sake.

The sound of bells chimed above the entrance doors as my father, uncle and Capt. Williams entered Miss Tomiko's alerting her to their presence. She raised her hands in surprise as she rushed over to greet them with a hug. It had been awhile since she last saw them- my father and uncle had become like family to her through the years. My father introduced Capt. Williams to Miss Tomiko as my uncle held up three fingers to her indicating that all three of them would be having the same usual food and drink.

"This is a nice little spot," said Capt. Williams as the smell of stir fried noodles and wine aroused his nostrils. "I see why you guys come here."

"Yep. The best damn yakisoba and sake you'll ever taste," my uncle replied as my father nodded in agreement.

The fresh smell of sake permeated my father's saliva glands as Miss Tomiko placed three small round cups and a teapot full of sake on their table. After filling their cups with sake, Miss Tomiko told them their food would be ready shortly.

"Damn! This sake is good," said Capt. Williams as he slowly sipped the drink slowly swishing the liquid around his mouth to absorb the full flavor. "I could drink this stuff all night."

"I told you that her sake taste great. Drink too much of it and you'll be floating on cloud nine," my father replied. "Wait till you taste the yakisoba."

A few minutes later, all three had their faces buried in oversized bowls eating yakisoba like there was no tomorrow. Miss Tomiko had commented that it was like watching three dogs eating- one would have their hand snatched off trying to take a bowl from my father, uncle or even, Capt. Williams.

"Man, either I was hungry or that yak was the best thing I ever tasted," said Capt. Williams.

"I told you," my uncle had replied. "Good enough to want to make you slap somebody."

After a few moments of burping and savoring the aftertaste, all three men held up their drinks and toasted Miss Tomiko for serving them such great food. Little did she know, her family would later start a multi-million dollar company that would produce such foods as Ramen Noodles, Tofu, Tempura and a host of other Japanese recipes.

"How are you feeling about this mission Doug," Capt. Williams asked, wanting to check on my father's state of mind.

"I'm anxious to get this over with; I've been thinking about everyone involved and the sacrifices that they are making. Even though it's not a battle zone, they can lose their lives if we're not careful," replied my father.

"Well Doug, one thing's for sure, your men are committed and will be more than ready. We got to be damn near perfect in our execution. The only concern I have is that if you will be able to identify your son- you've got to be absolutely sure. This will probably be our only shot at this."

"I know it's been a long time, but, I know my son. Don't worry, I will not make any mistakes."

Capt. Williams nodded at my father in reply as he motion for my uncle to join the conversation.

"I'm sure the execution will be 100 per cent. I have all the faith that Doug and his men will be successful. My only concern is that there are no guarantees that we'll find Freddy Jr.- the recon and Intel information says that there are kids around, but no one has been identified," said my uncle.

"It's a chance we've got to take Gill. I mean, I'm sure Doug doesn't want to look back on this with any regrets of not trying," replied Capt. Williams.

"I'm not saying that we don't try- I'm just saying that I wish there was a way to know for sure what babies were being held in that compound. I just don't want anyone to be disappointed, that's all," said my uncle as he looked at my father.

"Hey, I realize we're taking a risk. We're all faced with the fear of uncertainty. I've thought about calling this thing off numerous times. Before this all came about, I was settling on the fact that my son was a casualty of war and in my mind, he was already dead. But, when Earl brought this thing up, I couldn't help think that something supernatural was intervening- regardless of the outcome, it's a chance I've got to take, especially with the commitment from my men. I've never seen them this hyped to complete a mission- try telling them that we've changed our minds after all the running and staying up through the night."

All three men laughed knowing that they would face a lot of flak from my father's men if the mission was called off.

"Glad to hear that Doug," said Capt. Williams. "The plan is to run through the entire mission from start to finish over the next two nights and go live this Sunday morning."

"Sunday morning?!" exclaimed my father. "That's kind of quick ain't it? I mean, these guys just got into using the goggles and barely shot their targets. I think we need several more days."

"We don't have any more days to give Doug," said my uncle. "There have been some new developments with recon and the window of opportunity has shrunk. We've got to be ready to go Sunday morning."

Capt. Williams had explained that with new recon missions focusing on China, Sunday would be the deadline for them to attempt their own mission. He felt that my father's men would be ready on short notice even though my father had a valid point about needing more time using the infrared goggles. The next two nights would be challenging as tempers would flare, but only because they strived to be "perficio" in every aspect of the mission. It was now or never.

Chapter 24

THE NEXT DAY, EXCITEMENT STIRRED in the radio's announcer voice as he broke the news that the Beetles would be performing in Tokyo during the following spring to the delight of Capt. Williams. He was a big Beetles fan purchasing every record and album- he knew the words to every Beetle song. Little did he know that someone would make arrangements for him to meet the Beetles during their Tokyo concert and watch the concert from backstage. Capt. Williams' autographed albums and pictures from the Beetles would be worth a lot of money and a future entertainer named Michael Jackson would offer him millions for his collection.

"Hey Gill, the Beetles will be performing at the Budokan in Tokyo next spring," said Capt. Williams. "You know I've got to be there."

"I know you will. All those albums and records you got of them and most of them ain't even been opened or played. Man, you're seriously caught up in this Beetlemania hype," replied my uncle. "I just can't get into them."

Capt. Williams started singing a medley of Beetle songs to my uncle trying to get him to sing along. My uncle had spotted my father and his men approaching and motioned for them to come to his rescue. Capt. Williams gave my father a wink to play along as my father and his men joined him in singing to my uncle. After several minutes of singing, my uncle finally gave in and joined the others as he sang with them.

After a few minutes of singing, Capt. Williams gathered everyone together and instructed them to take a knee.

"Ok guys, here's the deal. Due to unforeseen plans, we have to be ready to complete this mission in a couple of days. This means that we have tonight and tomorrow to be 100 per cent. Remember, there can be no mistakes. I will be hard on everyone and we will stay throughout the night till we are perfect as a team. We have exactly 55 minutes to complete this mission from the time the helicopter lands, invade the compound, find the child and return to the copter. Do what you have to do to cover each other and make sure everyone returns to the copter. Again, I emphasized, we cannot leave any clues as to our presence in the area. Understood?"

"Yes sir," all replied.

"Good. Everyone in full gear with goggles on. It will be pitch dark in a few minutes. We will run this as if we're doing this for real. We will do this over and over again until there are no mistakes and we're under the 55 minute time limit. Ok gentlemen, let's go to work."

My father said that there was a man named Murphy who had a set of laws. He said that this night would be a prime example of one Murphy's Law: if anything could go wrong, it will.

My uncle had instructed all men to line up on the landing pad and timing would start on my father's cue.

"Ok guys, this is it. We need to concentrate and hit every detail. Upon my signal gentlemen," said my father as he held his hand up signaling my uncle to be ready to start the time. With all eyes focus on my father, he dropped his hand and took off running as my uncle started the time.

This is my Uncle Gill's account of what happened:

"I started the time when Doug dropped his hand and immediately, things went wrong. Two of the men tripped over each other causing a domino effect with the other men as they fell on top of each other. I could hear the frustration in their voices as they fussed among themselves. I could hear one of them say 'dumbass' and someone replied back 'your mama', which almost started a fight. Doug immediately reminded them that they were still being timed and for them to get their acts together. By the time the last man reached Capt. Williams, he had radioed to me that it took 18 minutes and asked what the hell happened. I replied that a couple of the men tripped causing a delay."

Capt. Williams picked up the conversation from this point:

"After the last man crossed over into the hangar, I was shocked to see the time of 18 minutes on their first run. After Gill told me what happened, I told them what the time was and they had to step up to complete the mission in 55 minutes. Their next step was to take out the 'dummy' snipers in the towers with one shot- everyone missed their target blaming the infrared goggles. At this point, I called off the practice in disgust telling them that they would've been killed if this was real. Bickering broke out among the men as I looked at Doug- all he could do was to shake his head as he yelled for the men to stop and look at themselves at how they were acting. Then came one of the most inspirational speeches I've ever heard during my lifetime."

My father to the best of his recollection along with Capt. Williams gave this account of his speech to his men:

"You call yourselves men of honor, men of duty and men of character called to defend their country. It doesn't matter whether we're black, white, yellow or brown- we all bleed the same color. It is our duty to protect the blood of each other- if one of us get shot, we all get shot; if one of us falls, we all fall; if one of us gets caught, we all get caught; if one of us gets left behind, we all get left behind; and if one of us dies, we all die. The body cannot move without legs, the body cannot see without eyes, the body cannot touch without hands, the body cannot hear without ears, the body cannot function without a heart. We all need each other to succeed- we are each other's eyes, hands, feet, ears, legs and heart. Divided we fall, but together we conquer. One is not greater than the other, but together, we are all great. It has been my pleasure to have you men under my command for you all have exemplified what brotherhood is all about: loyalty, trust, respect and unity. There is no failure in these qualities, which is why there is no failure in you- thus failure is not an option. This we defend."

Sgt. Johnson added the men's point of view after hearing my father's speech to them:

"After hearing what our leader said, we all looked at each other and I could see the focus and determination that was missing from our eyes. Capt. Williams had told us to go home and get our heads together for the next night- Sgt. Gill and Sgt. Douglas both left with Capt. Williams leaving us to gather our thoughts. The six of us stood in silence for a moment waiting for something to happen- it didn't feel right to leave. One of the men, Private Roland, left the group and headed toward the landing pad- seeing this, we all followed knowing that we had a job to do and as long as we had each other, it was going to get done. Once we all arrived at the landing pad, we all lined up putting on our infrared goggles. Private Roland held up his hand to signal the others to focus and start at the dropping of his hand. Once his hand dropped, we took off running toward the hangar being conscious not to leave anyone behind. There were no words spoken, no times taken- just the determination and commitment of being perfect in harmony. Once we entered the hangar, each of us took one shot at our targets and hit the bull's-eye. There was no looks of surprise, no shouts of joy, but an expectation of perfection in silence. We then covered our assigned housing units going through the motions of executing the enemy and then, covering the other units allowing time for the search of the baby as detailed in the plans we were told to memorize. After the counting down the allotted time, we all ran back toward the landing pad. We ran the exercise a couple of more times till we were perfect. Throughout the night, not a word was spoken- it was as though we read each other's minds. We've become the eyes, ears, hands, legs, feet and heart of each other. Perficio."

Three men hidden inside of a helicopter gave each other high fives as one of them shouted out 48 minutes flat. Capt. Williams, my Uncle Gill and my father had hid inside one of the helicopters after leaving the hangar. My father knew that his men wouldn't give up easily, especially after hearing the speech that was given.

"Damn Doug, how did you know that they were going to stay behind and work?" asked Capt. Williams.

"I know these guys. They hate to be defeated and told they can't do something. I just had to remind them of who they were and their purpose for being here. Now, they're ready," replied my father as he gave Capt. Williams the thumbs up.

"I second that," said my uncle in agreement. "Pity the enemy that have to fight these guys."

All three men sat back in the seats of the helicopter and for once, enjoyed the early morning sunrise before heading home- less than 36 hours before it would all be for real.

Chapter 25

A B-52 BOMBER FLEW OVERHEAD shaking the windows of my father's apartment waking him up in a startled manner as he looked out the window following the plane lowering itself toward the runway.

"Wow, a B-52 flying into Kadena," my father said to himself as he looked at the clock on the wall showing that it was 3 p.m. A B-52 bomber flying into Kadena usually meant that something was about to take place somewhere.

"Hey Gill," said my father as he called him on the phone. "What's with the B-52 coming into Kadena?"

"They've been flying in all morning man. You must have slept through the whole morning. Rumor has it that it has something to do with the OXCART mission into Communist China. I called Earl, but he doesn't know anything either," replied my uncle.

"It's not going to interfere with us leaving tomorrow is it?"

"No way brother. That's why we've got to do this tomorrow before OXCART takes over the skies next week. I told everyone to meet up at 6 p.m. tonight at the hangar."

"I'll be there."

The late afternoon sun reflected off the planes flying across the base generating a warm breeze around those in observance. The discharge of jet fumes from the planes created a mirage like image in the distance as more B-52's flew into Kadena landing at the nearby airstrip.

"What the hell is going on with all these B-52's," my uncle asked Capt. Williams as they were in route to the hangar.

"The latest I've heard that the B-52's are training for a bombing mission for North Vietnam in a couple of months. That's going to be some serious firepower," replied Capt. Williams.

"All of a sudden, Kadena has become a hotbed. You got all these planes preparing for recon missions into Communist China and now, B-52's coming in for bombing raids into North Vietnam. On top of that, I hear that the Prime Minister from Japan is coming to possibly meet President Johnson to ask that Okinawa be given back to Japan," said my uncle.

"Yeah, I heard that President Johnson may be coming to visit," replied Capt. Williams.

It was nearing six p.m. as Capt. Williams and my uncle arrived at the hangar. To their surprise, my father and his men were doing "walk-thru's" inside the makeshift housing units executing the enemy and searching for the baby.

"We must be late," said Capt. Williams with a smile.

"No sir," my father replied. "We came in early to go through the plan and cover all details."

Capt. Williams called everyone together to discuss the plan for the night's exercise and to finalize the itinerary for the following night. They would run through the entire mission making sure that each man knew his assignment and all details were covered. Capt. Williams had each man recite his role as he called out the steps in order of performance- they were perfect to the point of knowing what each other had to do and their location at all times. My uncle even called out random steps out of sequence to see if they knew what had to be done regardless of the order the steps were called out. My father and his men had all steps covered from the landing of the helicopter to taking out the snipers, searching and taking out the other men in their housing units, searching for the baby and the run back to the helicopter for takeoff.

"All right men, we can memorize well, but let's see if we can execute the "run through" the same way. Everyone line up at the landing pad with full gear on including your infrared goggles. You have 55 minutes to complete the entire mission from the time we land. Let's do this," said Capt. Williams.

My uncle would start the time on my father's steps and end the time on the last man returning from the hangar reaching the landing pad. My father reminded everyone that they were 24 hours from the real thing and this was no time for any mistakes as he motioned for my uncle to get ready to start the time. The time started as my father took his first steps toward the hangar with his men following. During the run, my father's mind drifted for a moment as he saw himself holding me after my birth looking over my body and checking all my fingers and toes. A smile spread across my father's face as his steps became faster and faster. A C-130 transport plane flying overhead snapped my father back into reality as he saw the hangar in front of him. He instructed his men to shoot their sniper upon arrival into the hangar and proceed with the rest of the mission according to plan. One shot was all that was needed to hit their target in the sniper tower as each man followed the steps of their plan in order. It was like clockwork as each man anticipated 2 or 3 moves ahead staying in sync with each other at all times not showing any signs of stress among them. After retrieving the "dummy" baby from the makeshift housing unit, they all ran the three mile distance back to the landing pad as my uncle stopped the time in less than 48 minutes.

"Forty-eight minutes is a great time given no obstacles. That will allow you seven extra minutes to clear any obstacles that stand in your way. Excellent job," said my uncle as he gave a saluted gesture to the men.

Capt. Williams radioed to my uncle to have everyone return to the hangar to review the final itinerary for tomorrow night's mission.

"I have never been more proud or impressed with the efforts you men have shown this past week. To take easily a two to three week training mission and to be able to learn and execute the details of the plan in five days is impressive. You men are what this Army is about and it is a shame that our country looks upon the color of your skin to define you instead of your heart and character," said Capt. Williams. "With that said, you guys are more than ready to accomplish this mission tomorrow night."

Capt. Williams, along with my Uncle Gill, spent the next couple of hours covering the flight plan, communications and alternative scenario plans in the event if they had to change details along the way. My uncle had distributed watches to everyone that had already been synchronized that would keep them on the same time. The flight plan was filed as a search and rescue-training mission, which Colonel Boyd had signed off and gave strict orders to Capt. Williams that upon completion of this mission, all documentation pertaining to this mission was to be destroyed without any traceable evidence that could link them to it.

"Go home and get some rest. We will meet here at 22 hundred hours to go over final details before boarding the copter. Remember gentlemen, this is a highly secretive and unauthorized mission- absolutely under no circumstances can anyone ever find out about what we're about to do, even if it means losing a life. Do we understand?" asked Capt. Williams.

"Yes sir," replied all the men in unison.

"Your watches are set- see you at 22 hundred tomorrow night," added my uncle.

All the men had dismissed and headed home for what would be a nerve-filled restless night of sleep. Everyone would be too excited to sleep like they should- they would all visualize over and over in their minds the scenes that would take place in less than 24 hours. Each man would be like a movie director, changing the script and outcomes of what could possibly happen during their mission. Some would play the hero saving the day while some would play the one finding the baby. It would definitely be a hard night's rest for them.

Chapter 26

THE HEADLINES OF THE SATURDAY morning base bulletin read, "American casualties mount as General Westmoreland authorizes more troops to Vietnam." My father continued reading the details of the troop movement and the deployment of the U.S. Marines, The U.S. Army and how Kadena and Naha Air Bases played a heightened role in the Vietnam War. Another two weeks, my father's platoon would be one of the first U.S Army units deployed to Vietnam. My father had said that you would think that he would be more nervous about Vietnam, but even Vietnam couldn't compare to the butterflies churning in his stomach of the mission that awaited him and his men in less than twelve hours.

This is my father's account of what he felt and went through leading up to the time of the mission:

"I had awakened that morning after only getting a few hours of broken sleep. I must have gotten up a hundred times looking out the window having conversations with the full moon lighting the nighttime sky. I had never been more nervous about anything as my anxiety kept my mind active reviewing whatever pictures I had of my son. My mind traveled back to the hospital where I was holding my son and remembering how he looked at me for the first time. I knew that I only had one chance at identifying my son if he was to be found and no mistakes could be made. The news of the troop movement and developments in Vietnam took away my anxiety for a moment as I thought about my platoon being deployed in a couple of weeks with mounting casualties being reported. From what I heard from others who experienced Vietnam, there would be no escape from death this time around- there was a chance that some of my men, including myself, may not return from this war. But, if I found my son, I had no choice but to return and be a father- my will to survive would even keep death on its toes to find a way to take my life. It would take more than a Viet Cong bullet to take me out. I was calling Gill to see if he saw the news about Vietnam, but it was he knocking at my door calling out my name as I hung up the telephone. I was glad to see him in person- when life became stressful, he had a way to make life easy with his words and laughter. He had come by to check on my state of mind and to see if I was just as excited looking forward to possibly seeing my son. He was already counting down the time noting that we had less than ten hours till we assembled. We had spent the rest of the afternoon watching a John Wayne cowboy movie and taking a nap as the wind blowing through an opened window caressed my face as the evening sun was starting to set. It was a fine time for me to finally drift off into a deep sleep as the time was fast approaching- the only sounds were of Gill's snoring and a couple of planes thundering in the distance."

A loud knock on the door awakened both my father and uncle as they both jumped up quickly looking at the clock on the wall showing 21 hundred hours.

"Oh shoot," said my uncle as he made his way toward the door. "I didn't realize it was that close to time."

Capt. Williams made his way inside tapping my uncle on his balding head and giving my father a fist to fist handshake.

"Are you guys ready or what?" asked Capt. Williams as both my father and uncle yawned at the same time.

"Oh yeah, we're ready," my uncle replied. "I got my stuff out in the truck. It'll only take me a minute to change."

"What about you, Doug?" asked Capt. Williams.

"I'm good. It'll only take a quick minute to get ready also," replied my father as he went into his bedroom to change.

"I figured we could all ride together and go over any last minute details," said Capt. Williams.

Capt. Williams had spent the entire day with a crew disassembling the makeshift compound inside the training hangar being careful not to leave any traces of their mission. He had assured Colonel Boyd that he would take responsibility for destroying all documentation and anything else associated with their secret mission. The filed flight plan listed them as an air recon search and rescue training mission- this too would be destroyed leaving no information ever being recorded for their particular flight. My father had mentioned that if Capt. Williams could cover up such a mission leaving no traces of their involvement, no telling what the U.S. Government kept hid from public records such as an airbase in Nevada called "Area 51", which Capt. Williams did say exists.

"All right guys, thirty minutes," shouted Capt. Williams waiting for my father and uncle to finish changing.

Five minutes later, both my father and uncle came out of the bedroom dressed in full battle gear looking ready for war. They all wore plain black uniforms with no insignia or patches that could identify them to the enemy. Capt. Williams had gone over a short checklist with them verifying the contents of their gear.

"Everything looks good. Let's load up," said Capt. Williams.

Some of my father's men were waiting outside the hangar where they had been training for their mission as Capt. Williams' jeep pulled up in front of them. The men had been reading an article about "Bloody Sunday", which detailed the Civil Rights Movement march on Selma, Alabama led by two men named Hosea Williams and John Lewis, how they were beaten, spat upon, called names and tear -gassed by Alabama State troopers. This also prompted other marches led by Martin Luther King and members of the Southern Christian Leadership Conference or SCLC.

"That's a bunch of bullcrap," said one of the men referring to the article. "We're fighting for our country and that's how they treat us."

They spent a few more moments reflecting on the article as Capt. Williams called everyone inside the hangar. Once inside, the men were amazed that the makeshift enemy compound was gone- everything was broken down, cleaned and even re-painted.

"Man, that's wild. You could never tell anything was done here," said one of the men.

"Good," replied Capt. Williams. "That's the way it's supposed to look."

"Ok men, listen up," said my uncle. "We have forty- five minutes before we board our helicopter. I need each one of you to check each other and make sure there is nothing on you that can identify us to the enemy. All jewelry and dog tags should be removed as well as personal identifications."

Each man proceeded to check one another uniforms and bodies to ensure there was nothing that could identify any of them as being U. S. military soldiers. Just like Capt. Williams, my uncle and my father, the other six were also dressed in plain black uniforms. After checking each other thoroughly, Capt. Williams handed each man an equipment checklist to make sure they had everything they needed for their mission, which included weapons, communication radio, infrared goggles and first aid. After the final checklist was done, they were ready to board their helicopter.

"This is it men. Remember, no mistakes- go over the plans in your head, we've got to have perfect execution," said Capt. Williams.

"Yes sir," replied all as each man checked and double-checked their lists and assignments.

One of the helicopter pilots came into hangar to inform Capt. Williams that the flight plan had been confirmed and they were ready for departure. Capt. Williams nodded toward the pilot and quickly introduced him to everyone.

"Perficio gentlemen, let's do this," said my uncle as they all headed toward the Huey helicopter with no identifying marks on it.

"Wow, is this a new copter?" asked one of the men as they entered and took their seats.

"Yeah, sort of- it's part of the new Huey's that arrived a few weeks ago," replied Capt. Williams.

There were four search and rescue-training missions scheduled to leave in fifteen- minute intervals and my father's team was the last copter to take off. No one in the control tower or for that fact, no one on base for the exception of Colonel Boyd, knew what was about to take place. Everyone involved had done their part to destroy all flight plans, maps and records to make sure that they were in complete secrecy about their mission. The United States or Japanese Governments would never have any records of what was about to happen. As far as the Air Force and Army was concern, this was a routine training mission to recover wounded soldiers and POW's. My uncle noted that if one could see the weapons being loaded, they would know that this was more than just a routine training mission- this was going to be a mini-war.

"R23, you are clear for lifted off," said the voice over the radio as the pilot gave a thumbs-up to Capt. Williams.

The starting of the engines startled everyone as the thunderous sounds of the blades slowly lifted the copter off the ground. Each man, regardless of their religion, prayed to a higher power as they all shut their eyes, feeling the vibrating power from the copter's engines kick into another cycle taking the Huey higher into the air.

"One hour and fifteen minutes till we land," said Capt. Williams as he instructed everyone to sync their watches. "We touch down at approximately at midnight giving us exactly till 12:55 to get back into the air. Remember gentlemen, we have 55 minutes to complete this mission. The way I see it, you have 15 minutes to get to the snipers, 20 minutes to search the compound and 15 minutes to get back to the copter leaving us 5 minutes to get back in the air before Japanese recon planes fly over. If you cannot find or identify the baby in the allotted time, you must leave and return to the copter within time- we have no extra time to give. Again, I reiterate, we cannot be identified or recognized by the Japanese. Shoot to kill to save our identities."

This is my father's account of his thoughts as they were in flight:

"The flight seemed to take forever as my mind wandered back to the birth of my son. It had been almost a year and a half since I last saw him and I thought about his first steps, what his first words were, if he resembled me and what name was he being called. I thought about how my son would react to me not knowing that I am his father. I also thought about what I would do if I couldn't find him or even identify him in the allotted time. At this point, I couldn't bare not leaving Japan without my son- I had a strong feeling that he was inside that compound and I was determine to find him. I looked at each of my men one by one and saw the determination and concentration on their faces- they would make sure my son would be found if he was there, even if it meant sacrificing their lives. I was proud of my men and wouldn't allow anything to happen to them if my life depended on it."

Chapter 27

"Fifteen minutes to landing," shouted the pilot over the loudspeaker.

Capt. Williams had instructed everyone to get their stuff together as they would hit the ground running. My uncle would keep everybody on time through radio communications while Capt. Williams would monitor the progress of the men by listening in on the communications.

"Five minutes till landing," shouted the pilot once again over the loudspeaker.

My father had looked at all the faces of each man- not one showed doubt, but were eager to bring the son of my father back home safely.

"Thank you all," my father said. "I owe you all."

"I believe I speak for all of us Sarge," said PFC Johnson. "It's our duty and honor. Just invite us all to his 18th birthday."

"You got it," replied my father.

The slowing of the engines indicating that the copter was making its descend as the pilot started counting down from 30 as each man put on their infrared goggles. The men were all in sync with the pilot as he was counting down from 10, 9, 8, 7, and etc.

"Go! Go! Go! Go!" my uncle shouted as the copter touched the ground starting the timer on his watch. One by one, each man rapidly jumped out and took off running toward their targets with my father bringing up the rear. My father would communicate with Capt. Williams as to the progress of his men making their move toward the sniper towers.

"All clear so far," echoed my father over the radio as my uncle called out that 7 minutes had passed.

The sniper towers were positioned just like the makeshift towers from the hangar. Fourteen minutes had passed when all the men were in position to shoot their assigned sniper.

"Number 1 aimed and ready," spoke the first soldier over the radio.

After all the others had radioed in with their targets aimed and ready to fire, my father gave the order on his three count to shoot their target.

"One, two, three," said my father over the radio as all six men fire their M-14's rifles in unison making it sound like a single shot was fired.

"Number one reporting, target down."

"Number two reporting, target down."

"Number three reporting, target down."

"Number four reporting, target down."

"Number five reporting, target not down."

There was another shot fired.

"Number five reporting, target down."

"Number six reporting, target down."

After all six men had confirmed that their targets were dead; my father gave the order for them to advance carefully to the compound and enter inside. My uncle called out 19 minutes for the search.

The compound was set up closely like Capt. Williams had designed inside the hangar during their exercises. There were four large hut-like housing units with a larger unit in the back area, which were the bathing and toilet areas. According to the instructions that were given, the children and women were in the first two units with the men occupying the last two units. The plan called for taking out the male rebels first as my father and his men quietly approach their units. My father gave the order for his men to split up in three's and take out the rebels. My father waited outside and served as a backup for both units in case help was needed. The men entered inside the units as all the rebel men were still asleep. One of the men held up eight fingers to indicate the number of men sleeping in the units. Being swift and quiet as possible, my father's men fired shots at the head of the rebel men and killed them all. This was considered a cruel execution style murder of defenseless men, but since this was classified as an act of war, it would be viewed as killing an active enemy.

"All dead in number one."

"All dead in number two."

"Fifteen minutes," my uncle had announced over the radio.

My father and his men advanced to the remaining two units where the women and children slept. He instructed three of his men to go in with him as the other three would stand guard outside.

"This is it," my father thought to himself as he entered the first unit.

There were women sleeping on one side while the children slept on the opposite side. My father signaled his men to be ready to shoot the women if they woke up as he shined his flashlight on the children. He had noticed that these children were older and didn't match my description. He signaled his men to exit as he followed them out.

"Number one negative," my father replied over the radio.

"Damn!" said my uncle upon hearing my father's report from the first unit. "I don't believe this is happening."

"They still got one more to search Gill. It's not over yet," replied Capt. Williams as he patted my uncle on his back.

"Doug, you got six minutes left," my uncle said over the radio as he looked at his watch.

My father looked at his watch as he motioned for the same three men to follow him inside the second unit while the other three kept guard outside. Upon entering the unit, my father scanned the children with his flashlight inspecting the faces of each child while the three men kept watch over the women ready to kill if they were awakened.

"I don't recognize any of them," my father said to himself. An eerie feeling came over him as he started to lose confidence in finding his son.

After checking a second time, he was convince that I wasn't present and gave up hope of finding me.

"Two minutes left, Doug," my uncle spoke over the radio.

"Hey Sarge," one of the men called out to my father. "There are two children on this side."

My father flashed his light on the other side quickly scanning the faces of the children. There were two babies that my father said could have resembled the son he was searching for. He picked up one of the babies and looked closely at its face and then scanned the body.

"Damn, I just don't know," my father thought to himself.

'Time's up Doug," my uncle spoke over the radio. "You've got to leave now in order to back it back on time."

My father stood staring deeply into the face of the baby he was holding in his hand.

"Sarge," said one of the men. "We've got to go or we'll be late."

My father had motioned for the three men with him to exit the unit and notify the other men outside to head back for the copter, as he would be shortly behind them. My father quickly picked up the second child and studied his face and body. He noticed some resemblance, but wasn't 100 per cent sure. Just then, he noticed something that gave him more reassurance as he wrapped up the baby and made his way toward the exit. Upon exiting, he felt a sharp pain on his right side- one of the women had stabbed him deeply with a knife.

"What the hell," said my father as he turned around and saw the woman coming at him again with the knife. He quickly raised his M-14 and shot her through the head. The other women had awakened at the sound of the commotion, but my father had already made his escape before they could identify whom he was or what he was. With blood dripping down his side, he made it out the compound as he started feeling light-headed, like he was going to faint, but he knew he had to hang on till he got back to the copter, carrying the toddler with every ounce of energy left in him- he was quickly losing a lot of blood.

"Where's Doug," asked my uncle as the other men made their return.

"He should be right behind us," replied one of the men.

"Hey Gill, we only got two minutes," said Capt. Williams. "The Japanese will be flying over soon."

"Doug, come in," my uncle called over the radio receiving no response.

"Damn, where is he?" said Capt. Williams looking at his watch.

This is my Uncle Gill's account of what happened during this time:

"With time running out, I knew that something was wrong with Doug. I radioed him several times with no response. Earl kept shouting that time was up and we had to leave- upon hearing this, Doug's six men jump off the copter and ran back toward the compound. I motion Earl to give them a minute as he instructed the pilot to start the engines and get ready to take off on his command. I could hear the nervousness in Earl's voice as he kept reiterating that we needed to leave before we all would be in a boatload of trouble. A few seconds later, about twenty yards from the copter, one of the men shouted that Doug was down and it looked like he had been shot. I immediately jumped off the copter and ran toward the crowd of men surrounding Doug. He was lying on his back going in and out of consciousness having difficulties trying to breathe. One of the men noticed that the right side of his uniform shirt was drenched in blood. I put my hand under his shirt feeling for the wound trying to ascertain if he had been shot as I felt an opened gash, which from a few months of medic training, seemed more like a knife stabbing rather than a bullet wound. Doug gained consciousness for a moment as he was trying to say something, but the words couldn't verbalize from his mouth. Not knowing how much blood Doug had loss, I knew that we had to get medical attention ASAP or he would die. With Earl shouting in the background to hurry up, I instructed the men to lift him off the ground and carry him to the copter. Doug, still trying to verbalize something, finally shouted out 'baby' as he pointed toward an area a couple of feet from where he laid. Thinking that Doug was disillusioned, I told him there was no baby and we had to leave immediately- we were already over our allotted time according to Earl and Japanese recon would be flying over in twelve minutes. As the men loaded Doug on the copter, he pointed back toward where he laid and whispered 'baby' again. One of the men yelled for me as I was getting ready to give Earl the o.k. to take off- it was Johnson who jumped off the copter and took off running toward the area where Doug was laying. I couldn't understand what Johnson had done as the rest of the men had jumped off the copter and ran after him. Earl was like 'what the hell is going on' as he looked at me as I was wondering the same thing. I jumped off the copter telling Earl that if we wasn't back in 60 seconds, go ahead and take off without us. I finally caught up with Doug's men as they were searching frantically for something. Then it dawn on me that Doug was trying to tell me that he had a baby with him and in the process of passing out, loss the baby somewhere around him. Finally, Johnson confirmed what Doug was saying as he came running toward us with a baby in his arms. I told everyone to high-tailed it back to the copter as I radioed Earl to get the copter up in the air. Two feet off the ground, I was the last one to jump inside the copter as Earl told the pilot to fly us the hell out of here like it was yesterday. Doug was unconscious, but still alive, as I looked at Johnson holding the baby."

"Sir, do you think it's him," asked Private Johnson, as he handed the baby to my Uncle Gill.

My uncle looked at the baby's face trying to see any resemblance to my father. He replied that it was possible, but he wasn't sure since initially, there didn't seem to be that much of a resemblance. My uncle thought to himself that my father founded a son- whether or not it was me was a different story.

Chapter 28

THE LATE AFTERNOON SUN BEAMED brightly off the bald head of my Uncle Gill as he stood up to take a stretch. We had all been wrapped up in the story of my father's journey to find his son and didn't realize that 8 hours had nearly slipped past us. The many empty cans of Colt 45 beer and ketchup soiled paper plates gave evidence to the passage of time as we all took turns using the only bathroom in the house. The clock on the wall showed the time of 5:30p.m., as my uncle reminded himself about an appointment he couldn't miss. He had told us that he was coming back with a surprise and not to continue with the story till he got back. After all these years, I now knew where the 3 inch puffy scar on my father's right side came from- he was always very reluctant to talk about this particular scar when asked, always saying that he got stabbed in war. Whenever I saw my uncle, he would always tell me that a price was paid for me and my father had the scars to prove it- I never knew what he meant by this, but now I started to know and see the price that was paid.

Capt. Williams had come out of house with a bowl of broiled peanuts that my uncle had brought from 'Charlie's Food Store', which was and still is a Sligh Ave. landmark in our old Tampa neighborhood. I became addicted to their Cuban sandwiches and deviled crabs which were the best in the area. After taking the first bite of his broiled peanuts, Capt. Williams would make several daily trips to Charlie's- he became addicted to them. While sitting in our backyard waiting for the others to return, I asked Capt. Williams to recount his version about the last few minutes before the helicopter took off- this is his account of what happened:

"We were in the danger of compromising our mission with only five minutes remaining till take off when Doug's men finally showed. Not noticing that Doug wasn't with them, I told the pilot to take off, but

Gill yelled to stop- Doug was missing. Immediately, butterflies filled my stomach as I lost my train of thought not knowing what to do with hardly any time left to do anything else. We waited around for a couple of minutes to see if Doug would show, but there was no sign of him. I told Gill that we were out of time and we had to leave. At that moment, one of your father's men jumped off the copter and took off running toward the compound followed by the others. Gill radioed your father, but there was no response. I told Gill again that we had no time for this- we were already three minutes over our time and I knew that if we didn't leave within the next couple of minutes, the Japanese would spot us. Gill told me to give them a couple of minutes and if they couldn't find him, we would leave. Both Gill and I knew that your father's men weren't going anywhere without him and they were prepared to fight as long as they could to save their leader. Fate was right on time when Roland yelled out that he found your father and that he was possibly shot. Gill immediately jumped off the copter and took off toward the area where Johnson shouted from as the others also raced toward him. I had no idea what was going on, but I knew that we had to leave immediately as I shouted out to Gill we were in the danger zone. A few seconds later, Doug was being carried by his men and while they were trying to place him into the copter, Doug kept pointing back toward the area of where he was found and kept trying to verbalize something, but his words were broken. I was about to tell the pilot to take off when Johnson jumped off the copter and took off running back toward the area where your father was found. By this time, my mind was gone- I could see Colonel Boyd tearing into my butt and all of us being court-martialed and thrown out. I looked at Gill like 'what the hell now' and he also had the same type look on his face. Gill then jumped off the copter and told me to take off in 60 seconds if he didn't return with the men. About 45 seconds later, Gill radioed to get the copter going as they were all on their way back. The next thing I saw shocked me as Johnson came running toward the copter holding a baby followed by the others. With the copter off the ground, Gill was the last one to jump in as I told the pilot to get us the hell out of here like his life depended on it- we were already seven minutes behind schedule. We barely escaped as our radar showed the Japanese recon planes slightly out of our range. Another minute longer on the ground would have spelled doom for all of us."

My father and Sgt. Johnson finally came out of the house carrying bags of chips with more beer and cokes, stocking the ice cooler for what would be a long evening of stories of the rescue mission and other events. My father had a portable T.V. on the patio as we all sat around watching reruns of 'Sanford and Son' while waiting for my Uncle Gill to return. My mother had called to say that she was still out with her friends visiting flea markets as was their customary ritual on the weekends. With the stuff that my mother bought, she could have opened up her own store- we had enough toilet paper, paper towels, and toiletry items to last for years and that's no exaggeration. At one time, I counted up 150 tubes of 'Close-up' toothpaste, 220 bars of 'Dial' soap, 60 bottles of 'Scope' mouthwash, 67 bottles of 'Vasoline' lotion, 350 rolls of 'Charmin' toilet paper, 245 rolls of 'Bounty' paper towels and numerous multitude of other household products.

The loud voice of my Uncle Gill alerted everyone to his return as he entered the backyard with a wide grin on his face.

"What the word Gill- you took long enough," asked Capt. Williams.

"I told you guys I had a surprise. I need all of you to close your eyes until I tell you to open them," replied my uncle as everyone closed their eyes.

There was a momentary shuffle of feet moving around with short bursts of giggling as my uncle told everyone to open their eyes.

"Oh my God!" exclaimed my father in shock.

"I be damn," added Sgt. Johnson.

"Oh heck!" said Capt. Williams.

All I could do was to look in amazement at the three men that my uncle had brought with him. With wide grins on their faces, the three strangers exchanged lengthy hugs with my father, Capt. Williams and Sgt. Johnson. It became a teary-eyed reunion as I was eager to find out who these men were and their relationship to my father. After a long few moments, my father finally introduced me to the men as they all looked at me in disbelief.

"Wow, I can't believe this is him," said one of the men.

One by one, my father introduced each of the men as we exchanged hugging handshakes.

"This is Robert Roland, Michael Nelson and Arthur Smith. They were part of the rescue team that retrieved you."

Sgt. Robert Roland was often referred to as "Rolly" and was the youngest of the group. Even though he was of Mexican descent, he considered himself part of the Black race and was always ready to fight if someone called him anything different. The years had been kind to Sgt. Roland still looking close to the picture taken in Okinawa- besides gaining a few pounds and grayish hair, he still looked in good physical shape with the muscles in his arm outlining the shirt he wore. I never expected to hear the words that proceeded from his mouth indicating that he had been around black people for most of his life.

"What's up bruth!" he said to me acknowledging me as a brother.

"I'm cool," I replied back, as we exchanged a series of rhythmic handshakes.

"Sarge, I can't believe this is your son," he said to my father while staring at me in astonishment.

"That's him," replied my father. "The one and only."

Sgt. Michael Nelson and Sgt. Arthur Smith were both alike in looks with both men having bulging bellies and receding hairlines. Both were tall over six feet and were heavyweight champions on my father's boxing team. My father had often referred to Sgt. Nelson as "Nellie" and Sgt. Smith as "Smitty". One thing I did noticed was that Sgt. Nelson had a limp in his walk causing him to use a cane. He later revealed that two bullets in his right leg from the Vietnam War nearly caused his leg to be amputated. The Purple Heart medal he received for being injured in battle wasn't worth the pain that he suffered every day from getting in and out of bed or being able to have an active lifestyle with his grandchildren. He said the pain can become so severe, that at times, he wished his leg was amputated.

Like my Uncle Gill, Sgt. Arthur Smith was a boisterous man who didn't have any problem telling "it" like it is when it came to the U.S. Army, the U.S. Government and his loyalty toward my father. Upon our introduction, he mentioned that my father saved his life in Vietnam. Sgt. Smith received head injuries from a grenade blast, which rendered him unconscious- my father, being injured himself, placed Sgt. Smith over his shoulder and carried him for many miles to safety waiting for the medics to pick them up. Sgt. Smith was adamant in showing me his scars on the back of his head, which looked like someone had engraved a set of miniature train tracks across the back of his thick cranium.

After all the introductions and pleasantries were made, my father had inquired how they came to Tampa, after not being able to find them previously.

"Gill got the number from my ex-wife and called me yesterday to let me know about the reunion," said Sgt. Smith. "I got in touch with Rolly and Nellie and after talking to Gill, we decided to surprise everyone by flying in today."

"Wow, this really calls for a celebration. I say we all go to MacDill-they got that seafood buffet with half-priced drinks," said my father.

Everyone was in agreement except for me- I wanted to stay and finish the story of my rescue, but I knew there was no chance of hearing anymore. Tonight would be filled with stories about families and missing friends accompanied by some of my father's and uncle's best buddies: Jim Beam, Jack Daniels, Bacardi, Chivas Regal and Seagrams.

Chapter 29

THE HILLSBOROUGH AVE. FUN LAND Flea Market was bursting with activity as vendors were quick to "wheel and deal" to sell their products and make their profit for the day. Among the buyers were my mother and me; I was intrigued by how my mother was known throughout the flea market and most of the vendors had their "special price" for my mother. This was a Sunday morning ritual for my mother as she would normally shop the flea market with some of her Japanese friends, but today, she had wanted me to come along to help carry the bundles of toilet paper, paper towels and other household goods. Despite only getting a few hours of sleep, I didn't want to disappoint her by not going as she would always look forward to me spending time with her. My father, my uncle and all their comrades had gotten stoned drunk the night before and I knew that my role was to be the designated driver making sure we all got home safe and sound. It was around 4 a.m. when I escorted five men separately to their rooms at the Admiral Benbow Inn: Capt. Williams, Sgt. Johnson, Sgt. Roland, Sgt. Nelson and Sgt. Smith. The smell of toxic liquor permeated from their bodies as I held my breath while laying each man on their beds. I knew that it would be late noon before they would rise back among the living. My mother had asked about what happened the night before and I told her that my Uncle Gill had located three of my father's men that were involved in my rescue and as a surprise, they flew in yesterday. We all had left for MacDill when my mother returned from her day of shopping with her friends wondering where we all were.

"How far did they get with the story," asked my mother.

"We stopped at the point where they were boarding the helicopter after my father had been seriously injured and one of the men recovered a baby," I replied.

"Ok. Still not come to me yet. No matter what is said, I always love you as my own and protect you the best I know how."

"I love you too. As far as I'm concerned, you're the only mother I have and you've always been there for me."

I had wanted to ask my mother more questions about her involvement and if she knew Mitsuko, but I decided to wait until the story got to that point. We had spent the rest of the morning browsing through the multitude of vendors- we had found one particular vendor who had numerous collections of baseball cards and comic books. I was amazed at the value of the baseball cards especially when he showed me a Mickey Mantle card worth over a hundred dollars. From that day on, my mother became an avid card collector amassing enough cards that would fill one bedroom and would be valued into the thousands of dollars. Her passion of card collecting would also spill over into porcelain statues and China doll collections.

I quickly ran into the house to answer the phone as I looked around to see if my father and uncle were up from their sleep.

"Hello?" said the voice on the other end. "This is Earl. I'm calling to see if someone can pick us up."

"Hey Capt. Williams, this is Freddie Jr." I replied looking at the clock flashing 1:30 p.m. on the wall. "I don't know where my father and uncle are right now, but I can come pick all of you up."

"That would be great. I need to stop at that Woolworth's department store to get some things."

"No problem Capt. Williams. I'll be there in thirty minutes."

I had already known that my father and uncle were still sleeping as I looked through the house for them. The smell of fouled liquor filled the guestroom as my father and uncle were still sleeping on the bed. I shook them both trying to wake them, but to no avail, they barely missed a snore.

"Hey wake up, the house is on fire," I said loudly, clapping my hands in their ears.

My uncle opened his eyes and grabbed his head as he tried to focus his attention towards me.

"What the hell," said my uncle. "The house is on fire?! Hey Doug, wake up- the house is on fire."

My father jumped out of bed with a dazed look on his face.

"What? What are you talking about?" asked my father.

I told my Uncle Gill and my father that everything was fine and that it was the only way to get them up. I informed them that the others were ready to be picked up from their hotel and that I was on my way to get them.

"You guys seriously need to shower- you smell like gin and doodoo," I said pointing to the both of them.

"We probably do. I feel like poo and I probably pooted on myself," replied my uncle as he headed toward the restroom.

"Give us about an hour before you get back with the guys. Take them through a tour of Ybor City and let them see the sights," said my father as he was using his hand to shield the brightness of the day from his eyes.

Sgt. Smith was standing outside smoking a pipe as I drove up in front of his room- I could smell the strawberry aroma coming from his pipe making me want to take a puff. Sgt. Smith sensed my attraction to his pipe and immediately told me that smoking a pipe was not good for my health. He said that the strawberry aroma was to cover up the dash of marijuana mixed in the tobacco which help eased his symptoms from the exposure of the "Agent Orange" chemical used in the Vietnam War by the U.S. Government. Not being familiar with Agent Orange, I asked Sgt. Smith to explain it to me. This is his account of the U.S. involvement with the "Agent Orange" chemical and its effect on him:

"The damn government didn't even have the nerve to tell us that we were risking exposure to chemicals during our fight in the jungles of South Vietnam. Agent Orange was an orange mist chemical released by the U.S. Government through the Air Force- I believe they called it Operation Ranch Hand. The chemical was suppose kill the crops in the jungle consumed by the enemy and drive them out to help U.S. ground forces take control. But, the Government failed to disclose the harmful effects of the chemical to civilians and soldiers who were exposed. Cancer along with other diseases caused from the exposure led to many illnesses and even death among the civilian population of South Vietnam and ground forces of the U.S. and Vietnamese military. Our government told us not to worry and that the Agent Orange chemical was safe toward humans. After retiring in 1971, my body started going through a lot of changes and I had troubles breathing as well as experiencing piercing pains throughout my body. The

Veterans Administration Hospital told me that there was nothing major wrong with me and that Agent Orange had nothing to do with the way I was feeling. They gave me some pills for high blood pressure and told me to exercise regularly and not to drink so much, but I know the pain I was feeling was real and since they didn't give me something to ease my pain, I came up with my own remedy using my pipe. The U.S. Government kept denying that Agent Orange had anything to do with the illnesses suffered by veterans of the Vietnam War, but I heard recently that studies showed that exposure to Agent Orange can cause cancer and other diseases. They don't give a damn about us- it just amazes me that colored troops were mostly exposed. They got what they wanted out of us and now they don't want to do a damn thing to help us. As far as I'm concerned, it's just another cover up by our government for experimentation of the chemical on colored troops. They knew that exposure would cause cancer and kill us."

Capt. Williams and the others finally came out after watching reruns of Prince Charles and Princess Diana mass wedding ceremony.

"Man that was some wedding. Too bad the marriage won't last," said Capt. Williams.

"Why you say it won't last," asked Sgt. Nelson.

"Prince Charles is a player. He loves women too much to be dedicated to just one and besides, he's still young. But, I tell you what though, Diana would do me just right."

"Her butt is too flat for me. You know I like mines plump and juicy," said Sgt. Smith with a sly grin.

It was funny hearing these old war veterans talk about women as they were trying to educate me on the fine art of being a "player" and on the sensitive parts of a woman's anatomy. After listening to their expertise on women, we all finally packed in the car and headed out.

"Nice ride. You got that "Starsky and Hutch" thing going on. Real nice," said Sgt. Roland as he gave me a slap on the back.

"Thanks," I replied.

Remembering that Capt. Williams needed to stop at Woolworth's, I pulled into parking lot of Eastgate Shopping Center and directed Capt. Williams to the store. Sgt. Johnson and Sgt. Roland decided to pay a visit to the Walgreen's package store to purchase some refreshments for the day.

"Man, its sure is hot here," said Sgt. Smith wiping beads of sweat from his face.

"What's a Zayre department store," asked Sgt. Nelson as he was reading the marquis display of all the shops in the plaza.

"It's like a Woolworth's in a way, but bigger," I replied listening to the radio announcer saying that it was 95 degrees.

It was perfect timing as Capt. Williams, Sgt. Johnson and Sgt. Roland all came out at the same time, all carrying bags of items. I could smell that Sgt. Johnson and Sgt. Roland sampled some of the refreshments as their breath fill the surrounding air with gin. After gathering everyone in the car, I mentioned that I was going to take them to Ybor City to look at some of the sights, which to me, wasn't a whole lot to see. Ybor City was considered an historic neighborhood with the cigar factories and shops being the focal point. There were some Cuban restaurants and a couple of entertainment clubs- this area of Tampa had been neglected for a long time and was just beginning to be rebuilt. The population of Ybor City consisted mostly of Cuban and Spanish immigrants who came to Tampa as workers in the cigar factories. Ybor City helped label Tampa as Cigar City, but more importantly, Ybor City became known as the cigar capital of the world.

"Not much action during the day," said Sgt. Roland as he was reading some of the advertising signs written in Spanish.

After a brief drive through Ybor City, we headed toward the ghetto part of Tampa, which my father called the "projects" and where he grew up as a boy. This was the 22nd street area- I could remember my father always jokingly telling me to duck my head whenever we drove through this part of Tampa for fear of gunshots. The low income housing units looked unlivable as little black kids were playing in the sand and chasing each other. Babies were running around in muddy looking diapers crying for someone to pick them up. Elderly looking women were sitting on stacked milk crates and trash cans playing cards on a makeshift cardboard table supported by concrete blocks and spitting snuff into paper cups. The sound of loud music echoed from one of the bars as we drove past a crowded group of people dancing around holding liquor bottles in one hand and cigarettes in the other.

"What's up my people," Sgt. Johnson yelled out through the window of the car. "Shake that booty!" Sgt. Roland added as he was getting excited over the gyrations of one of the women moving her hips around. "I tell you what though, I don't care what city you're in- you can find some fine women in the projects."

"Yes you can," I replied, having encountered a few fine shapely girls at my high school from the projects.

Continuing our drive through 22nd street, Capt. Williams noticed several baseball fields, but particular, the name of the fields: Belmont Heights Little League. Having coach little league baseball, he inquired if this was the same little league group that won a string of Little League World Series.

"Yes it is," I answered. "In fact, one of my classmates, Dwight Gooden, pitched on one of those Little League World Series Championship teams." Dwight Gooden would later be drafted by the New York Mets as he dominated the Major Leagues as a rookie and lead the Mets to a World Series Title.

"Wow, that's cool," replied Capt. Williams.

We had turned off 22nd street onto Sligh Ave. toward the house when Capt. Williams yelled for me to stop. I thought something was wrong as he pointed toward the sign that read "Charlie's Food Store".

"This is my place. Hey guys, you've got to try their deviled-crabs and broiled peanuts. I'm addicted to them."

In the short time that Capt. Williams had been in Tampa, he had gotten to know the employees of "Charlie's" on a first name basis and took a picture with the owner, Charlie, which he autographed for Capt. Williams. After buying all the deviled-crabs and boiled peanuts, Capt. Williams and the others came out of the store and loaded up the Torino. I figured that my father and uncle had enough time to freshen up as we were less than a couple of minutes from the house.

The smell of fried chicken and cornbread greeted our noses as we pulled into the driveway of the house. My mother, peering through the kitchen window, gave us all a wave and shouted to us that my father and uncle were in the backyard. Listening to jazzy sounds coming from the radio, my father and uncle were flipping through old photo albums looking at pictures from the past. My father was holding up a newspaper article from the Florida Sentinel Bulletin, which was a black owned Tampa newspaper covering events and news centered on the black community. The article talked about the return of my father to Tampa from Okinawa- attached was a photograph of my father, mother and me, which he passed around.

"Nice looking family Doug. Glad that everything worked out with Marco. She was a good choice," said Capt. Williams.

I gave Capt. Williams a dubious look wondering what he meant by his remark concerning my mother. My father nodded his head in agreement and sensing my apprehension about Capt. Williams' comment, he told me that there was still more I had to find out and that I would understand why that particular comment was made by Capt. Williams.

My mother, speaking to my father in Japanese, told him that the food was ready. Sgt. Nelson and Sgt. Smith were bringing in the bags from Walgreen's as my father yelled that the food was ready and for everyone to proceed to the kitchen to fix their plates. My mother had everything laid out like a buffet as each man was lined up waiting to fix his food.

"Man, this smells good," said Sgt. Smith as he looked at the spread of fried chicken, collard greens, macaroni and cheese, rice and cornbread. Sgt. Smith had tasted the chicken and reached over and gave Sgt. Nelson a soft slap across the back of his head.

"Hey man, what was that for," asked Sgt. Nelson.

"Sorry about that Nellie. The greens taste so damn good, I just had to slap someone," replied Sgt. Smith with a grin on his face.

Everyone had paid compliments to my mother for her cooking as they finished eating their last little bit of food. Sgt. Nelson reminded everyone that beer was on ice in the backyard as we followed his lead out the back door. Sgt. Smith fixed up his "special pipe blend" and began to smoke as my uncle lit one of his Cuban cigars. My father tossed everyone a beer except for me, giving me a RC Cola. After giving time for everyone to relax, my father suggested that we continue the story of my rescue from where they left off.

"I don't remember where we ended at," said my uncle as he motion for me to remind them.

"Y'all had just made it back to the helicopter. My father had been injured badly and was unconscious and Sgt. Johnson retrieved the baby," I replied as I took out my notepad, which I recorded some key points of the conversations that had taken place.

A Lonely Teardrop

As I stand on the edge of time
I often wonder why I'm here
In a place that's passed its prime
Sitting in this cold atmosphere

Where has everyone gone dear sir
That I might be left feeling blue?
Wondering when I can stand like a tree of fir
Becoming a body with a clue

Injustice was served on this day
With innocent cries heard from a mile
Can you comfort me like they say
With your gentle touch and smile

Don't cry for me in your heart
For everyone will mourn in the night
Just like the soul that plays its part
I will not go down without a fight

To the one who suffers in pain
I will give you no reason to fear
For in just a little while you will gain
The hope that comes in a lonely tear.

Chapter 30

"Damn Gill, is he going to make it?" asked Capt. Williams as he looked at my father.

"Looks like he's been stabbed pretty badly- he's losing a lot of blood. I got pressure on the wound now. You better get in touch with Colonel Boyd," replied my Uncle Gill as he had a look of uncertainty in his eyes.

Capt. Williams had instructed the pilot to have Colonel Boyd on line once they got in range. Colonel Boyd had instructed Capt. Williams to radio him asap if something out of the ordinary happened. Scenarios had previously been discussed about what course of action to take if something like what happened to my father took place. Once confirmation of escaping the Japanese recon was confirmed, Colonel Boyd was to be contacted concerning any other incidents. Plans were already outlined and would be initiated by Colonel Boyd's command.

"Sir, I have Colonel Boyd on line," said the pilot to Capt. Williams.

Grabbing the headset from the pilot, Capt. Williams informed Colonel Boyd what took place and confirmed to him that there was no trace of their identity by the Japanese.

"How bad is he hurt?" asked Colonel Boyd.

"He's unconscious at the present, but more important sir, he's lost a lot of blood," replied Capt. Williams.

"Ok Captain, as soon as you land, code blue will be set to go," replied Colonel Boyd.

Colonel Boyd had arranged for a medic group to be on standby in case medical attention was needed. The doctor in charge had owed Colonel Boyd an immense favor and agreed that there would be no records of any medical emergency resulting from this mission. As far as the Colonel was concerned, this would be recorded as a military training accident shall the need arise to explain this incident to any superior officers. Capt. Williams had reiterated to everyone to keep silent and any questions should be referred to him if the need arose. It was Capt. Williams' responsibility to make sure there was no evidence of this mission and to destroy any records including medical emergencies.

"How's the baby doing," asked Capt. Williams as my uncle was looking over the baby's body.

"He looks ok," replied my uncle. "Nurse Nancy should be ready at the hospital to receive him once we arrive."

The silent question that was floating in everyone's mind "was this baby Doug's son". My uncle seemed to be reading everyone's mind as he blurted out, "I don't know gentlemen, I don't know. I mean, he could be. Something had to tip Doug off."

The pilot notified everyone that they would be landing in a few minutes. Capt. Williams reminded everyone that tonight was a "seek and rescue" training mission and nothing else. Each man's story had to corroborate each other in case an issue ever came up concerning what took place with them or my father. As the helicopter made its descent toward the landing pad, my father's men placed themselves in position to transfer him off the copter and into the hands of the medics. As soon as the copter landed, my father's men quickly unloaded my father and placed him into the ambulance. There was another private vehicle, which transported my uncle and the baby to the hospital. Capt. Williams and my father's men stayed behind to perform the "cleanup", which included destroying all flight records and paperwork- it would be as though this mission never existed.

"Is the surgery team ready to go?" asked the lead doctor addressing one of the nurses.

"Yes sir. We're set to go with the x-rays," replied one of the nurses as a team of medics carried my father on a stretcher into the surgery room. "Colonel Boyd is in the observation room."

My father kept fading in and out of unconsciousness as he was being prepped for surgery. One of the nurses informed the doctor that x-rays revealed a three-inch stab wound on my father's right side, which stopped short of puncturing his lung.

"His pressure is dropping-vitals are below norm," said one of the nurses.

The doctor and nurses immediately performed surgery procedures to stop the bleeding along with giving my father an infusion of blood. During the surgery, Colonel Boyd, observing through the viewing window, was amazed at the precision that the medical team was working. He saw monitors, IV's and surgical instruments being hooked up in a matter of minutes as they began performing on my father. After the completion of the surgery, which took a couple of hours, the doctor met with Colonel Boyd, who was waiting in the doctor's office.

"What's the word doc?" asked Colonel Boyd.

"Well, one thing I can say, Sgt. Douglas is a lucky man. Another centimeter and his lung would have been ruptured," replied the doctor.

"Meaning?"

"Meaning that he might not have survived. He's loss a lot of blood. If it wasn't for someone's quick thinking to put pressure on his wound, he might have gone into severe shock."

"What's the prognosis for his recovery?"

"Depending on his body, it can take two weeks to thirty days. But, I should know more in 48 hours."

The conversation was interrupted by loud voices outside the infirmary near the recovery rooms as several nurses were trying to stop my father's men from coming inside. Colonel Boyd and the doctor came out of the office to see what all the commotion was about. One of the men spotted Colonel Boyd and immediately called for everyone to be at attention.

"At ease men. What's going on?" asked Colonel Boyd.

"Sir, we just want to find out how Sgt. Douglas is doing, sir," replied one of the men. "The nurses won't tell us anything."

"We were told not to reveal any information concerning Sgt. Douglas," said one of the nurses.

"It's ok. These are Sgt. Douglas' men," replied Colonel Boyd. "Doc will fill you guys on his condition."

After getting the doctor's report, the men felt at ease as they saluted Colonel Boyd and the doctor as well as apologizing to the nurses for any misunderstanding. Colonel Boyd had congratulated the men on their mission and asked about the package, referring to the baby.

"We're on our way to meet with Sgt. Gill. He's been with the package since we arrived," replied one of the men.

"I will check with Capt. Williams and Sgt. Gill later on," said Colonel Boyd, as he saluted the men and headed out of the infirmary.

Nurse Nancy had finished her examination on the baby as my Uncle Gill was anxiously waiting in the viewing room of the maternity ward. He still was uncertain if my father grabbed the right baby wondering what my father would do if that was the case. Capt. Williams had made his entrance as Nurse Nancy came in from the examination room.

"What's going on?" asked Capt. Williams, as he nodded his head at Nurse Nancy.

"The baby is going to be fine. Just some scratches on the arms and legs," replied Nurse Nancy.

Both Capt. Williams and my uncle were both relieved to hear what she had said. The footsteps of my father's men echoed down the hallway indicating their approach as Capt. Williams asked my uncle if the baby was my father's.

"Right now, I don't feel confident we have the right child," said my Uncle Gill, looking perplexed.

"Damn, what do you mean we don't have the right child- Doug said he was absolutely sure that he could identify his son," replied Capt. Williams.

"I know what he said Earl, but I don't see any resemblance. This child should have some of Doug's features- especially coming from a black man."

"What are we supposed to do then?"

"I don't know."

The doors of the viewing room swung open as my father's men made their entrance. They had informed Capt. Williams and my uncle as to the condition of my father and that Colonel Boyd wanted to meet with them later. My uncle informed the men that the baby was fine, but there were still questions concerning if the right baby was retrieved. Capt. Williams couldn't believe that all they had gone through might have been for naught: the time and effort that went into covering up the mission from the Army, U.S. and Japanese governments- they had committed cold blooded murder and major crimes for nothing even though the killings were classified as an act of war. Then there was my father, who nearly loss his life and was lucky to be alive.

"No way!" exclaimed Capt. Williams. "The boy has got to be Doug's son."

"I'm not saying that he's not Doug's son. Nurse Nancy said that they usually take footprints at birth, but there are no records of his birth on file. It's possible that Mitsuko obtained all the birth records before they left the island. If that's the case, we got more problems coming. We've got to talk to Doug," said my Uncle Gill as he held his head in his hands.

"But, if we have the wrong child, how do we tell Doug the mission was a failure? That will devastate him, Gill."

"I know it will. The question is what do we do with this child if it isn't Doug's?"

There remained an unsettling silence in the room as Capt. Williams, My father's men and my uncle stood frozen like statues wondering what to do next. This is Sgt. Roland's account of what went through his mind at this time:

"All I could think of was that our Sergeant was near death and Capt. Williams saying that we had the wrong child. I knew that Sarge wouldn't just randomly grab a child just for the sake of taking if it weren't his son. My emotions almost got the best of me as I was on the verge of telling Capt. Williams that he didn't know what the hell he was talking about. I was the one who put my M-14 in the middle of a young boy's forehead and shot him- what will haunt me forever was the look he gave me before I pulled my trigger. His eyes were that of a pleading soul begging for his life- I had to close my eyes as the bullet entered his forehead and splattered his brain. I couldn't shake that scene from my mind even though the Army classifies this type of murder as an act of war. There would be many more scenes like these during our tour in Vietnam, but none like the one of the eyes that still haunts me."

"Ok men, go get some rest. We'll inform you if there are any sudden changes with Doug. Again, despite the circumstances, job well done," said Capt. Williams, remembering that they were only three hours removed returning from their mission.

"It's 0800 already," said my uncle. "I'm going to sit with Doug for a while in case he wakes up."

"Call me if anything happens. I'm going to brief Colonel Boyd on everything. For some reason Gill, I got a feeling that this is a start of a can of worms that we wish we didn't open," replied Capt. Williams.

My uncle shrugged his shoulders at Capt. Williams- this was one of the few times that my uncle was speechless. A few moments later, Nurse Nancy came back into the room to let my uncle know that the baby was sound asleep and that he was also potty trained as she observed him using the restroom on his own.

"So, what are you calling the little fella?" asked Nurse Nancy.

"Well, I guess we can call him Freddie for right now," replied my Uncle Gill. "I'm on my way to see Doug to see how he's doing."

My uncle had started to ask Nurse Nancy if she thought that Freddie had any resemblance to Doug, but thought better of it, not wanting to leak out any details of what took place earlier. Nurse Nancy was a good friend of my Uncle Gill and on occasion, even dated a few times, but they were too different in personalities and race. My uncle had once gotten a death threat for dating Nurse Nancy, a white woman- they felt it best to remain friends to avoid any racial conflict between them and others.

"I'll let you know if anything happens on this end," said Nurse Nancy as she waved my Uncle out the door.

"Thanks for everything Nan," replied my uncle as he exited the door with many questions lingering on his mind.

Chapter 31

THE DOCTOR HAD REPORTED TO my uncle that my father was recovering better than expected despite having a knife stop short of rupturing his lung. It would be a couple of weeks before my father would be back on his feet and into rehab to strengthen his body.

"Good to hear doc," my uncle said. "Is it ok to see him now?"

"Oh sure. He's sleeping now. The effects of the anesthesia should wear off in a few hours, which he should awaken then," replied the doctor.

My uncle had spent the next few hours watching my father sleep as he thought about what he was going to tell him concerning Freddie. How could he tell him that the child he grabbed wasn't his or that his son wasn't even in the compound. Maybe my father was desperate enough to grab a child not wanting the mission to be a failure. My uncle's mind became a cinema as many parts of the mission replayed over and over trying to justify all the unlawful events that took place. The drumming sound of my uncle's fingers thumping on the armrest of the chair kept in rhythmic beat of the heart monitor attached to my father as my uncle sat in observance. The attachment of tubes and IV's made my father's condition seemed more graved than what it was; if it had not been for the doctor telling my uncle that my father was recovering better than projected, one would describe him as being near death. My uncle had once said that my father was a fighter who fought not to keep himself alive, but fought to keep the hopes, dreams and visions of the Negro soldier from being snuffed out by racism, hatred and war. Meanwhile, my uncle was in deep thought thinking about the different scenarios that could take place if it was confirmed that my father had grabbed the wrong child. This is my uncle's account of what was going through his mind:

"I was convinced that Doug had grabbed the wrong child and I was even to the point of saying that Freddie wasn't even there. I couldn't understand why Doug would grab a child not knowing if he had positive identification on his son. There had to be something that led him to believe he found his son, whatever it was, I don't know. My concern at the moment was how we were going to explain where this child came from if he wasn't Doug's. Earl was right when he said a lot of questions would be raised concerning the child- I just hope that Earl had all the answers, especially since there were no records of anything. I had an eerie feeling that someone or something would expose us. Then, there was Doug's injury- his unit was to be deployed to Vietnam in a couple of weeks and there was no way he would be ready to go. I had to believe that Doug had reasons for taking the child that he did. Even if the child was Doug's, we still had obstacles to be cleared to get his son back into the U.S."

It was nearing sunset as my uncle woke from a deep sleep still slumped in the chair in my father's room as it was his first chance of sleeping since coming from their mission. He glanced over at my father who was surprisingly staring back at him- he was trying to speak, but the tubes coming from out of his mouth wouldn't allow the vocals cords to make a sound.

"For once, I don't have to hear your mouth," said my uncle letting out a laugh.

My uncle said that he knew by my father's facial expression that he had a few questions to ask, the main one being about his son.

"Hold still a minute Doug while I get the nurse to see if she can get those tubes removed so you can talk," said my uncle.

A few moments later my uncle had returned with a couple of nurses as they started examining my father. After examining him, the nurses confirmed that all vital signs were stable and saw no problem in removing the tubes from his mouth.

"Once your doctor confirms that it's ok to remove the tubes Sgt. Douglas, we'll be back to take everything out," said one of the nurses. The nurse had informed my uncle that it might be about an hour or two before the doctor would make his rounds to check on my father.

"I'm going to go home and take a shower and grab something to eat and then I'll be back," said my uncle as he looked at my father. "Man, you need to take a shower too."

My uncle went on to crack a few more jokes about my father saying that he might as well take advantage of the situation since my father couldn't come back with any cracks about him. My father recalled this moment from the best of his memory about what was going through his mind during this time:

"My vision was slightly blurred as I saw Gill standing over me saying something, not being able to hear exactly what words were coming from his mouth. It sounded like a thousand voices echoing inside my head as I tried desperately to reply back, but something was keeping my mouth shut as I felt air being pushed down into my throat. I didn't know where I was or what happened to me- the last thing I remembered was running through a wooded forest with my son in my arms heading for the helicopter. I didn't even remember making it back to the helicopter. I heard Gill saying something about nurses and I assume I was in a hospital. I could hear a beeping noise in the background as I thought about my son and tried to speak, but again, I couldn't force my vocal cords to make any sounds. I wondered if my son was alive as I was hoping that Gill would give me some confirmation as to his whereabouts instead of talking about junk I didn't want to hear. My body felt paralyzed as I tried to raise my hand to get Gill's attention, as it felt like a ton of bricks holding my hand down. I heard voices talking as warm soft hands rubbed my arms and legs and one of the voices said something about being stable and taking tubes out of my mouth. Then a second gentle voice said something about changing the bandages on my side as she informed me that I had surgery for a knife wound and that I may feel some pain as the anesthetics start to wear off. I then remembered that I had been stabbed on my right side as I left the housing unit with my son. All I could think about was for someone to please tell me if my son was alive and where he was. One of the nurses told me to relax as she was giving me a sedative to help me rest and mentioned that my doctor would see me shortly. That's the last thing I remembered as I saw Gill leaving the room."

Shades of dark clouds hovered over the base indicating that a storm was fast approaching as my uncle looked up into the sky and saw a B-52 making its landing on the runway. The skies in the background were filled with fabulous displays of lightning streaks as loud thunder rumbled the base with earth-shaking sounds. This was typical monsoon season for Okinawa as scenes like these became common from week to week producing massive amount of rains and an occasional typhoon from time to time. Soft raindrops tickled my uncle's head as he entered his apartment rushing to answer the ringing phone.

"What's the latest Gill?" asked Capt. Williams on the other end.

"Doug's doing fine. He was awake when I left. The doctor should be removing his breathing tubes this evening so that he can talk and move around," replied my uncle.

"What about the child?"

"The child is doing fine as well. Nancy will call me if there are any changes."

"Have any determinations been made as to the identity of the child- is he Doug's son?"

"I'm not sure. I plan on asking Doug when I go back if he's absolutely sure that the boy is his son. There had to be something that alerted him to this child."

"Do you want me to meet you there," asked Capt. Williams.

"If you want- looks like we got some bad storms coming through. I may wait until it blows over," replied my uncle as static erupted over the phone from a lighting strike nearby. "We've better get off Earl before we get shocked. I'll call you when I'm headed toward the hospital."

Large balls of hail pounded the rooftop of my uncle's apartment as the rains intensified with the thunder and lightning making their presence felt throughout the island. He had compared the pounding of hail to someone fiercely beating a pair of drumsticks using his roof as a set of drums.

"This ain't no joke," said my uncle referring to the hail.

He had prepared some candles for lighting just in case the electrical power went out overnight. My uncle took a chance on calling the hospital to check on my father and to let the nurse know that he wouldn't return until the weather cleared. The nurse replied that my father was doing well and that some of his men had came by to see him. She suggested to my uncle to wait until morning to come back out. If there were any drastic changes she would call him immediately. With that being said, my uncle turned off the remaining lights and slipped into his bed listening to the pitter-patter of raindrops putting him to sleep, as total exhaustion overtook his body leaving no thoughts or dreams behind.

Chapter 32

THE AGITATED SOUNDS OF BUZZING chainsaws welcomed my Uncle Gill from his peaceful night of sleep as he cracked his eyelids to see a glimmer of sunlight peering through his window.

"Aw shoot, it's too early in the morning for all that noise," said my uncle, as he grabbed for his watch, which read 7:25 a.m. He looked through his bedroom window and saw several work crews cutting branches from a tree that had fallen overnight from the storms. Recognizing one of the men on the work crew, my uncle called out to him through the window and asked if any major damage had been done on the base. The man replied that there was no major damage except for trees and some debris from rooftops lying in the streets. My uncle commented that as always, the work crews were doing a great job and gave them a salute.

The ringing of the phone caught my uncle's attention as he made his way to the kitchen to fix himself a cup of coffee. It was one of the nurses from the hospital calling to inform my uncle that my father was looking for him.

"Tell him I'll be there in thirty minutes," said my uncle as he thought about what to say to my father concerning the mission. After a hot steaming shower, he quickly got dressed and headed toward the hospital.

"Not bad," my uncle thought to himself as he observed the minimal damages left by the storms. The road to the hospital was all clear for the exception of a couple of stoplights not working.

My uncle had stopped by the nurse's station to get a full report on my father's condition. The nurse had informed him that my father was doing well and that the doctor had the tubes removed from his mouth.

"He ate some soup and was able to go to the restroom on his own," said the nurse.

123

"Sounds like he's recovering pretty well," replied my uncle as he thanked the nurse for the update and headed for my father's room.

"Well I be damned- the dead has risen," my uncle said as he entered my father's room seeing him propped up in his bed and fully awakened.

"What took your butt so long to get here," replied my father in a weak sounding voice.

"Shoot, you didn't hear the rains last night? The thunder and lightning was so bad that I thought the world was ending," replied my uncle.

"Man, I didn't hear Jack. I slept through the whole thing. The doctor came in early this morning to examine me and made me get up and walk. He says that I have to walk every four hours to circulate my blood."

"Well, it's good to see you're up. How's the body feeling?"

"I'm sore on my right side, but other than that, I feel good."

My uncle knew the questions were coming as he tried to distract my father by focusing on other topics of conversation, but it was short-lived as my father quickly asked him about the child. My uncle said that the child was doing well and that Nancy was taking care of him.

"Doug, there is one question I need to you to answer," said my uncle.

"Yeah, what?" said my father as he sense an uncertainty in my uncle's voice.

"I don't know how to say this, but I don't think that child is your son. I want to believe he's your son, but I need to know what made you pick him."

My father took a moment to gather his thoughts as doubts surrounded his mind by what my uncle had said. My father had thought about the men who almost sacrificed their lives for him along with all the help from Capt. Williams and Col. Boyd to pull this mission off without any major problems. He thought about the great lengths that were taken to cover everything from the U.S. and Japanese Governments and if founded out, they all could be in the trouble fighting for their lives. My father's mind had drifted back to when I was born as he spoke to my Uncle Gill.

"When Freddie Jr. was born, we both watched him as the nurses were cleaning him and checking his body and vitals. After they completed their exam, you recalled the nurse handing me my son?"

"Yes," replied my uncle not knowing where my father was going with his statement.

"I looked over his body and noticed that he had a birthmark on the right side of his back. Well, it's the same place where I have a birthmark also. When we were in the enemy compound, I noticed that the last child I picked up had the same birthmark. Gill, I remembered that birthmark from his birth and knew that he was my son."

"Wow," replied my uncle with a smile.

"Go check it out just to make sure I wasn't seeing things. I mean, I want us to be a hundred percent sure."

"I'm going to see Nancy in a moment. I'll stop back by and let you know."

As my uncle was leaving the room, Capt. Williams had made his entrance as he greeted my uncle and updated him on what was going on and my uncle updated him on my father's condition. After their brief conversation, my uncle left Capt. Williams with my father as he made his way on the other side of the hospital where Nurse Nancy was working in the maternity ward. My uncle thought about what my father had said about the birthmark as he felt a renewed confidence in my father's judgment.

"What's going on Nan?" said my uncle as he saw Nurse Nancy changing a newborn's diaper.

"Oh, hey Gill. What you no good?" replied Nurse Nancy.

"I came by to check on Freddie and I was hoping to spend some time with him."

"Sure Gill. I'll get him in a moment for you. He cried quite a bit last night, but other than that, he's eating well."

While waiting for Nurse Nancy to get Freddie Jr., my Uncle Gill took a moment to look at the babies in the maternity ward noticing that most of them looked alike. He wondered if my father could pick which baby was his son among the many that were present without hesitation. Even though my father told him about the distinguishable birthmark, he still wasn't quite convinced that the right child was taken.

"Here you go Gill," said Nurse Nancy as she handed Freddy Jr. to my uncle.

"He looks a little different," said my uncle as he noticed the slight tan skin color and defined slant eyes.

"He's just been eating well. He is a little undersized for an 18 month old baby, but he's starting to fill out."

My uncle started doing the gibberish nonsense talk making the baby laugh along with blowing fart sounds on his stomach.

"Another thing Gill- he is speaking Japanese," added Nurse Nancy. "I've been teaching him simple English words."

My uncle had raised the t-shirt of the baby and noticed the birthmark that my father had described giving him confidence that my father was right about the baby being his son.

"Hey Nan," said my uncle, "Do you think this baby looks like Doug?"

"No doubt about it," replied Nurse Nancy with a confident tone.

"What makes you so sure?"

"Apparently, you haven't changed his diaper yet."

"What's that got to do with him being Doug's son?"

Nurse Nancy tossed a clean diaper to my uncle and instructed him to change the baby.

"C'mon Nan, what's the purpose," my uncle said as he laid the baby on the changing table and proceeded to unpinned his old diaper. "I mean, how's this suppose to prove that he's Doug-." My uncle couldn't finish his sentence as he stared in amazement with his eyes wide opened. "Well, I'll be damned. Now I know he's Doug's son."

"Uh huh. Now you know," said Nurse Nancy. "What Japanese baby has a dark colored penis- one of the parents has to be black."

My uncle's latest discovery was what he needed to see to finally convince him that my father had found his son.

My Uncle Gill gave this account of what he was feeling at this time:

"When I saw his penis, I was both flabbergasted and relieved. Just to prove her point, Nan showed me several other Japanese- American babies fathered by white men and had me compared the color of their penises to that of Freddie's and she was right on cue. Freddie had to be fathered by a black man and Doug was his father, especially with both of them having identical birthmarks on the back of their right shoulder area. I couldn't wait to tell Doug that he truly found his boy. The mission was justified and everything we did was now forgivable. I could now live with this part of my life without guilt knowing that a father found his son and I had a nephew. Doug's men would be relieved to know that they succeeded in bringing home the son of their leader- it was all worth it as they would witness the tears of a father as he would thank them for everything. Capt. Williams and Colonel Boyd would both be just as excited to know that we succeeded in bringing Freddie home. As the weeks and months went by, Freddie started to look more like Doug and at times, during certain facial angles, the resemblance was uncanny. Doug was able to communicate to Freddie both in English and Japanese- sometimes starting a sentence in one language and finishing it in the other."

A week had passed since my father's surgery and he was well beyond the doctor's expectations of recovering. He had been walking around the hospital ward several times a day and the deep cut wound was healing better than expected. Capt. Williams and Colonel Boyd had stopped by on several occasions to check on him, keeping him abreast on the upcoming deployment of his unit to Vietnam. My father tried to convince Colonel Boyd that he would be ready to deploy with his unit, but the Colonel wouldn't hear of it, especially without the doctor's clearance. The doctor told Colonel Boyd that even at the rate my father's speedy recovery, he would need an additional 2 weeks of rest and rehab before being considered for deployment. My father was a soldier and the leader of his platoon and couldn't imagine not leading them into battle. But, there would be unforeseen issues lurking on a different battlefield that my father would have to deal with before being deployed to Vietnam to join his men.

Chapter 33

It had been a few days since my father was discharged from the hospital as he met with his men on the eve of their deployment for Vietnam. He had assured them that he would join them as soon as possible and told them to protect each other lives. Sgt. Roland gave this account of this time period:

"Our leader had come by to give us some words of encouragement as well as instructions on protecting each other. We were all nervous about going to Vietnam- we've heard about the mounting casualties of American soldiers and we knew that there was a strong possibility that some of us wouldn't survive. We still didn't understand why we were being sent to Vietnam or why we were involved in this war. To make matters worse, we were being led by a white sergeant who didn't know anything about us nor didn't give a damn about our unit. It had been said that this white sergeant made a comment about not wanting to lead a bunch of niggers into combat and we all would be killed quickly. Anyway, our sergeant told us not to fight this war for America, but fight it to keep each other alive and protect our platoon. Sgt. Douglas gave each one of us a hug. It became very emotional as he pointed at every one of us and said 'this we defend' saluting the platoon.

Very early the next morning, my father looked up into the skies as the roaring engines of the transport planes flew overhead carrying soldiers headed for Vietnam. The thought of not being with them tore my father apart inside- after leaving his men the night before, he made a last ditch effort to Colonel Boyd to allow him to join his men, but was denied. This would be the first time that he would be separated from his men in battle- they were a precision fighting unit defining what a combat unit should be like despite the color of their skin.

My Uncle Gill had driven up and saw my father looking at the planes flying overhead. He knew what was going through my father's mind and knew that there was nothing that could be said to put his mind at ease.

"They'll be alright Doug," said my uncle as his voice caught my father's attention.

"I should be with them," replied my father as the last of the transport planes flew out of his view.

"Earl called this morning and said that he needed to see us. I told him we would meet him at Miss Tomiko's place for breakfast.

Hearing Miss Tomiko's name brought a smile to my father's face. It had been a long time since he had seen her and missed her cooking.

"What's going on with Earl?" asked my father.

"Not sure. He just said that we needed to talk," replied my uncle. "Is Freddie still over at Nan's?"

"Yeah. I dropped him off last night. She's a lifesaver Gill. I think she's grown attached to him"

"Well, that's a good thing considering that she offered to keep him in case you had to leave for Vietnam."

Over the past weeks, my father and uncle had numerous conversations about who would take care of me while my father was away in Vietnam. Nurse Nancy had volunteered to keep me, but my father left my uncle as my guardian; my uncle had promised to look after me and take care of me if my father didn't return from Vietnam.

The smell of fried tempura, fish and eggs made my father's stomach rumble as my uncle pulled in front of Miss Tomiko's place. Capt. Williams was already inside waiting for them and told Miss Tomiko that her favorite customers were coming to eat breakfast. She prepared a special breakfast for them as she anxiously waited for them to walk through the doors.

"That smells good," my father said as he entered through the doors and walked toward the cooking area where Miss Tomiko was waiting with a smile. He gave her a bear-squeezed hug and a kiss on the cheek as she laughed in excitement. My uncle followed up with a hug and a kiss also as they exchanged greetings in Japanese. She instructed them to sit at the table with Capt. Williams- their food would be out shortly. All three men exchanged handshakes as they sat down staring at Miss Tomiko bringing their food to the table. The aroma of the eggs and rice intoxicated the taste buds of all 3 men as they looked like dogs getting ready to attack a piece of meat.

"Man, this is what I'm talking about," said my Uncle Gill.

The next half hour produce sounds of smacking lips and finger licking as all 3 men ate their plates clean leaving only the fish bones. The fresh hot sake wine was the final touch to a delectable breakfast as my father rubbed his stomach expressing his gratitude for the fine cooked meal.

"Seriously, we need to open up a restaurant back in the states and have all of Miss Tomiko's recipes," said my father. "I bet we can make a ton of money."

"Ok Earl," said my uncle, "What's going on that we had to meet this morning?"

"We got some issues that have come up. The Japanese Government has made an inquiry with our government concerning an event that took place over 3 weeks ago. It seems that someone invaded an underground compound executing the men and that a child was taken. The Army has sent a communiqué asking our department to investigate. Fortunately, I've been assigned to investigate and to file a formal response to government officials."

"I thought that this was all covered up Earl," said my uncle. "How did they know what happened?"

"It seems we were not out of their recon range. They picked us up, but they don't have any identifiers as to who did it."

"What does this mean Earl?" asked my father.

"As far as I know, no one has any knowledge of what we did. Remember, Colonel Boyd's name is to stay clear of this matter at all cost. But, it does leave us with one problem and that is why I wanted to meet you both. One thing that I fail to take into consideration is explaining how Freddie all of a sudden appeared back on base after being missing for nearly 18 months. There are no birth records or any records on Freddie- it's going to be hard to get him out of the country without paperwork."

"Why do we need paperwork? He's my son. I don't understand Earl," replied my father in astonishment.

"We know he's your son. The problem is explaining who the mother is. Your son is recognized as being Japanese since the mother is Japanese and according to the laws of Japan, he is a Japanese citizen and cannot be taken out of the country unless the mother consents by signing the proper documents. Also, we cannot involve the Army or our government because they have no knowledge of what we did and if they find out, it would be the end of our careers and even prison. Whatever we decide to do, we will be on our own."

Butterflies had fluttered my father's stomach after hearing what Capt. Williams had spoken. His mind was still trying to process what was said as he gave a glance of confusion toward my uncle, who was just as confused.

"I still don't see what you're getting at Earl. I mean, are you saying that Doug can't take his son out of Okinawa?" asked my uncle.

"Exactly."

"So, what are we supposed to do Earl?" asked my father.

"There are a couple of options. One thing that is working in our favor is that there is no proof as to the identity of your son's mother. You're due to be deployed to Vietnam to join your troops in a couple of weeks so that leaves a short time to have something done. I have a plan that may work, but it may be something that you'll be against. And if so, the only other option is to leave your son in Okinawa."

"We can scratch leaving him here- what's the other option?" asked my father.

"It's unorthodox, but the only other alternative is to find a Japanese woman that you can marry and claim as your son's mother. I can have all the paperwork prepared and have a birth certificate made. If you want to do this, you got a week to find a woman to marry and who is willing to keep your son."

"This is crazy. You're saying that I got to get married this week? That's insane," replied my father.

"I got to agree with Doug, Earl. There's got to be another alternative," added my uncle.

"There is none," said Capt. Williams.

This is Capt. Williams' recollection of the conversation that took place and what happened during this time:

"A few days before meeting with Doug and Gill, I received a phone call from Colonel Boyd asking me to pick him up from his office. I knew something was wrong- I hardly ever picked up Colonel Boyd unless something was wrong. I picked him up from his office and he told me to drive off base to our regular fishing pier where we would go fishing. Colonel Boyd told me that Central Army Command informed him that the Japanese Government made a formal inquiry as to the ambush of an underground Japanese compound. The inquiry he showed me stated that men were murdered and a child was missing. It also stated that a Japanese recon plane caught a glimpse of a helicopter in the area, but had no positive identification of the helicopter. Colonel Boyd told me to take care of it and file a formal response as well as making sure that nothing in the future could be linked back to us. I assured the Colonel that nothing could trace this incident to us especially since there wasn't a positive ID on the copter- it could have been anyone. I knew right away that Doug's son could present a problem since he all of a sudden showed up after being reported missing for nearly 18 months. Questions were starting to circulate around the hospital, but Nurse Nancy managed to quell all suspicions and keep Freddie Jr. out of the limelight of discussions. I met with both Doug and Gill and presented them with what Colonel Boyd had shown me and gave them options on what we needed to do to permanently put this situation to rest. I knew that Doug wouldn't go for leaving his son behind, but I didn't know if he would be desperate or crazy enough to go with the only viable solution, which was to marry a Japanese woman in a week's time. I had the connections to put everything into play if Doug chose to go with this choice- he only had to find a woman to marry. Both Doug and Gill looked at me like I was crazy when I told them that this was the only viable solution- there was nothing else that could be done. No matter the decision or outcome, it was my responsibility to keep Colonel Boyd and the men that were involved from being at risk and exposed, even if it came down to jeopardizing the loss of Freddie Jr. to keep my word to Colonel Boyd."

There was a silence among men as my father stared into the morning horizon watching the rise of an easterly bright sun making its way across the early morning sky. The sounds of seagulls celebrating their mouthy catches of fish intertwine with my father's thought processes as his mind was slowly digesting what Capt. Williams had revealed to him and what needed to be done to save his son as well as all the men who were involved with the rescue. With his deployment of Vietnam looming near, my father was already facing fear and pressure with mounting American casualties including the loss of a couple of his own men. Now faced with having to find a wife in a week's time only added to the woes that was already starting to discombobulate his mental state of mind, he knew that leaving his son was not an option.

"Damn. Crap on top of crap. Where the hell am I going to find a wife in a week?" said my father with a sigh.

"There are ways Doug. American dollars will buy you a wife temporarily. Once you get out of Okinawa and back to the states, you can get a divorce and send her back to Okinawa," replied Capt. Williams.

"How much money are we talking about?" asked my Uncle Gill.

"A hundred or two could do it. I would recommend finding a family in need and pay half now and the other half when you send whoever is your potential wife back to Okinawa," replied Capt. Williams. "I'd be willing to contribute to the cause."

"Now the question is where am I going to find a wife. I mean, I don't just want to marry anybody. But, since this is short notice, its first come-first serve," said my father.

"Well then, I suggest we wrapped things up here and let you and Gill get started on your wife search while I start working on the documents needed. I also need to prepare a formal response to the Japanese Government as to their inquiry. Keep me posted," said Capt. Williams.

The morning sun was quickly approaching high noon as all three men took one last drink of their sake before leaving Miss Tomiko's. She had refuse to let them pay their tab for the food and as always, my Uncle Gill left her a 10 dollar bill on the table-they all exchanged hugs with Miss Tomiko and exited to the outside world. Capt. Williams jeep become a like a mirage in the distance as my father and uncle watched till the jeep was no longer in sight. A cackling sound from a nearby rooster filled the air around them as my father looked into the sky wishing for some sort of divine intervention to save the day. His days turn into hours, hours into minutes and minutes into seconds as he glanced at my Uncle Gill waiting for him to make a suggestion on what to do next. Instead, my uncle pointed toward a fishing boat for rent and walked toward it with my father following behind him.

"It's a good time to go on the waters and drop some lines. We need to just get away from everything for a moment and let nature talk to us.

Nothing like the peaceful serenity of fishing to put one's mind at ease," said my Uncle Gill.

A few minutes later, a small-framed Japanese man guided the fishing boat into the open waters as the afternoon sun greeted the faces of my father and uncle as they savored each touch of the comforting breeze coming from the sea.

Chapter 34

THE PHONE KEPT RINGING AS my father hurriedly entered his apartment to answer it talking to the phone as if it was an animated object brought to life.

"Hold your rings Mr. Telephone, I'm coming," said my father.

"Hey Doug, I need you to meet me at the fishing boat that we took out yesterday. I think I might have found a solution to our problem," said my Uncle Gill.

"What do you mean?" replied my father.

"I'm talking a possible wife for you. We need to hook this thing up now if we're going to make this happen quickly."

"But, but, this is too quick. I just came from seeing my son over at Nancy's and I don't know if I can just rush into something like this. I mean, what if it doesn't work out Gill- what's going to happen to my son if I'm not here?"

"Don't worry brother- I got you covered. I'll be here and so will Nancy. But, we got to seal this deal. We got more than us at stake Doug."

My father's mind reverted back to the conversation from the previous day at Miss Tomiko's when Capt. Williams informed them about the Japanese inquiry and that careers could be at stake as well as the loss of a son.

"I'll be there shortly," replied my father in Japanese.

My Uncle Gill was admiring the morning catches of fish being displayed on the docks as my father drove up and honked his horn. My uncle motioned for my father to join him on the docks as he pointed to an octopus that was having its tentacles cut and clean. Octopus tentacles were a delicacy among the Japanese and tasted good when cooked correctly.

"Look at this! This is the first time I've seen an octopus cut up and cleaned," said my uncle as he gave my father a hugging handshake.

They both took a moment to observe the expertise of the Japanese fishermen slicing, dicing and washing the parts of the octopus. My father said that it was like watching a surgeon perform surgery on a body as the fishermen were displaying their cutting skills and doing different tricks with the knives they were using. Upon seeing my father and uncle, one of the fishermen stopped his cutting and made his way to them. He was like most Okinawan men, very short in stature with silky smooth graying hair and black slanting eyes, small nose and a small mouth. His age didn't reflect his youthful aurora as it suggested that he was in his early forties- my father and uncle both were shocked when they found out this Okinawan fisherman was 60 years old.

"Doug, this is Masao Tokumori," said my uncle as he made the introductions in Japanese. "He has a daughter that is in her mid-twenties and she works at the Post Exchange. I was referred to him by one of my contacts and we can possibly work something out with him."

My uncle had brief Mr. Tokumori of the situation at hand prior to my father's arrival and worked out a preliminary solution that would mutually benefit everyone involved. My uncle quickly brought my father up to speed on the details of the plan as he spoke both in English and Japanese translating back and forth between Mr. Tokumori and my father.

This is my father's recollection of the conversation that took place and the events that unfolded:

"Gill had explained that Mr. Tokumori had a daughter named Yoshiko who worked at the Post Exchange on the base and he'd be willing to approve of her marriage for the right price along with a few minor stipulations. The price was 300 American dollars and the stipulation was that once Yoshiko and I were settled in the States that I would fly her back to Okinawa with some American made items that Mr. Tokumori wanted. I would pay him 200 dollars upfront and give Yoshiko 100 dollars when she flew back to Okinawa. I would also agree to have the marriage dissolved under military exceptions as well as pay for any expenses for Yoshiko such as clothing, medical and anything else she may need. Gill also included the fact that Yoshiko would have time to bond with my son, as she would have to claim to be the mother and keep him during my tour in Vietnam. Gill had done a good job in working out all the details and all that was left was for me to meet Yoshiko and get married. Gill also informed Capt. Williams to start the paperwork process as well as contributing the 200 dollars needed for Mr. Tokumori. I didn't expect Capt. Williams to pay the entire 200 dollars, but Gill said that it was more money than we had and that Earl came from family with money. I had made a pledge to myself that I would pay Earl back the 200 dollars at a future date and I even made Gill promised me that he would pay Earl if something was to happen to me in Vietnam. With all parties in agreement, Mr. Tokumori would talk to his daughter about the arrangement, which she would be in cooperation, not knowing that it would be the end of her life in Okinawa as she knew of it."

"Hey Doug, we can run by the PX and catch a glimpse of Yoshiko if you like or you can wait till later once Mr. Tokumori sets everything up," said my uncle after they had left Mr. Tokumori.

"I guess that would be alright. At least I can see what she looks like," replied my father as he jumped in his jeep and followed my uncle back toward the base.

The commissary and post-exchange were full of service personnel and civilians doing their weekend shopping as bagboys were competing with each other to assist shoppers to help carry their bags to their cars for a quarter, dime or nickel tip. My father and uncle managed their way through the scurrying crowds till they reached the Post Exchange entrance where lines of people were waiting for their purchases to be checked out by the cashiers. My uncle took a quick glance at the cashiers ringing up their customers as he noticed one of the cashiers wearing a nametag, which read "Yoshiko."

'There she is Doug," my uncle said as he pointed to a young woman with long black hair.

"Where? I don't see her," replied my father as he was trying to follow the direction of my uncle's pointing finger.

My uncle took a moment to focus my father's eyes on Yoshiko, as she was busy conversing with one of the service personnel about their purchases.

"Not bad Gill," said my father. "Not bad at all."

"She looks nice Doug. Better than what I expected. I think she'll do just fine."

"We'll see Gill. I'm still a little leery about jumping into this thing so quick. I wish I had more time to get to know her- everything's happening so quickly."

"It's not like you have a choice Doug. We got to make this happen to keep everybody and everything protected."

After a half hour of observation, my uncle and father agreed that Yoshiko would fill the role needed for their plan. My father felt butterflies in his stomach- a feeling that he hadn't felt in a long time, even going to Vietnam didn't make his stomach feel this queasy.

"Go get some rest Doug. I got to help Earl tie up some loose ends with paperwork," said my uncle, as he gave my father a slap on the back.

"Ok. I guess I'll see you later. I think I'll go grab my son," replied my father, taking one long last look at Yoshiko.

"I'll drop by later," said my uncle, as he waved his hand in front of my father snapping him out of his staring trance.

The long afternoon sun reflected bright rays of light from the seas nearby as my father arrived at Nurse Nancy's apartment to pick me up. There was a bond starting to form between us as she would always cuddle with me at night and play with me during the day. She taught me simple English words such as water, ice, pee-pee and basic colors. She had even thought about asking my father to adopt me if something was to happen to him during Vietnam, but she knew that my Uncle Gill was my guardian in the absence of my father and would never allow me to be departed from him. My uncle would take me as his own son and would raise me as one of his own if it came to that scenario.

"How's he doing Nan," asked my father, as he picked me up in his arms.

"He's doing just great. He now knows the basic colors in English," replied Nurse Nancy.

She proceeded to hold up colorful objects and asked me to identify the color as she pointed to them. One by one, I would rattle off the colors of the objects she was holding up as my father looked in amazement.

"Damn, that's great Nan. In just the short time you had him, he's really picked up on English and especially being able to recite his ABC's."

"He's real smart Doug. You should put him in school as soon as you can."

"Yeah. But I got to get through some other issues first. Hopefully, I'll have everything worked out by next week before I leave for Vietnam."

Not wanting to explain the particulars of his comment, my father quickly gathered up my sleepover bag, picked me up and headed toward the door.

"Thanks for everything Nan. I should be ok with him tonight. If I need you to watch him tomorrow, I'll call you," said my father.

"No problem Doug. You know where to reach me," replied Nancy.

After a few hand waves of good-bye, my father drove away following a formation of planes overhead headed toward his apartment.

"Airplane!" I said, pointing skyward toward the planes.

"That's right son!" my father replied in delight. "Airplanes."

My father nodded his head in amazement, giving his son a rub on the head, as a smile came across his face- he knew then that he had to do whatever was necessary to keep us together.

Chapter 35

MY UNCLE GILL WAS WAITING patiently outside of Capt. Williams office as an exchange of voices seem to be finishing their conversation with echoes of good-byes in Japanese vibrated through the slightly cracked door. Four unrecognizable Japanese men, escorted by Capt. Williams, made their way outside carrying stuffed envelopes.

"What's going on Earl," said my uncle, as he followed Capt. Williams back into his office.

"Just taking care of some business with my Japanese contacts," replied Capt. Williams.

"Gotcha," said my uncle, knowing that Capt. Williams made a pay-off for some information and documents.

"Is Doug squared away with everything," asked Capt. Williams.

"Yeah. I made all the arrangements with Mr. Tokumori and we will be meeting with him later tonight or tomorrow morning," replied my Uncle Gill.

"Good. I've got the documents from my Japanese contacts and all the paperwork from our side is almost completed."

Capt. Williams gave this account of what took place during this time:

"After the meeting at Miss Tomiko's, I contacted a Japanese friend of mine who was well connected with the Japanese Government and told him that I needed official divorce documents drawn up between Mitsuko and Doug as well as family information on Yoshiko Tokumori to help track down her family members. Gill had informed me about Yoshiko when he saw her at the PX and asked her some questions- he found out that she was single and Gill thought that she would be a good match for Doug. After my contact gave me information on Yoshiko's family, I relayed the information to Gill that her father lived in the village near the base. Gill went to go track Mr. Tokumori down at the fishing docks and through some of the local fishermen, found him. Gill had spent the day explaining Doug's situation to him and after hearing the story, Mr. Tokumori was against the idea of his daughter marrying a complete stranger coupled with the fact that Doug was a military man and black. But, after a few drinks of wine, a couple hundred American dollars and some stipulated points, Mr. Tokumori gave his consent to arrange the marriage. Around that time, it was customary for the father or eldest son to make the marriage arrangement for their daughter or sister. Gill contacted me afterward and told me that everything was a go from Mr. Tokumori. From that point, I started the paperwork process for everyone, including documents showing Yoshiko being the mother of Freddy Jr. All that was left to do was for Doug to agree to the arrangements and sign all the documents necessary to complete this transaction. A couple thousand dollars was split between several contacts to make this happen with the understanding that no questions were to be asked and the all forged documents were to be recorded and stamped with the Japanese Ministry of Government Affairs. I took care of having all documents completed by the U.S. Army between Mitsuko and Doug dissolving any relationship. This was a costly cover-up, but it was well worth the price as the Japanese and U.S. Governments closed their file on the inquiries for nothing was ever found."

Fighter planes performing aerial maneuvers escorted in the late evening sun as my father and I were observing them from outside of his apartment. The thunderous sounds of the plane's engines drowned the sound of my Uncle Gill's jeep as he pulled up behind us and startled our ears with his horn.

"Checking out the maneuvers, huh?" said my uncle.

"Yeah. Little Freddy is fascinated with planes. I bought him a toy plane and that's all he wants to play with- every time he hears a plane flying over, he runs to the window," replied my father.

"Sounds like we might have a future pilot."

"He's smart too, Gill. Nan is doing a great job teaching him English. To be almost 2 years old, he knows his ABC's and can count to 100."

My Uncle and my father watched for a moment with smiles on their faces as I was running through the grass with my arms spread apart imitating an airplane and making airplane sounds. My father, as if reading my uncle's mind, asked him about the meeting with Mr. Tokumori and his daughter, Yoshiko.

"That's why I'm here Doug. Mr. Tokumori will be ready to meet with us in about an hour."

"One hour?" my father asked, as a lump escaped his throat and exploded into butterflies in his stomach. He wasn't ready for this meeting to happen, but knew that he had no choice if it meant risking the loss of his son along with the careers and livelihood of the men who were involved in the executions or "an act of war" as Capt. Williams put it, to rescue his son. He owed it to Colonel Boyd, Capt. Williams, my Uncle Gill and his men to marry a complete stranger to make all suspicions disappear. Capt. Williams had paid the money to have the supporting documents made and to have any second thoughts were out the window.

"Mr. Tokumori has talked with Yoshiko and everything is a go. She understands that this is only temporary and the money is needed for her family."

"I guess I'll be ready. We have to drop little Freddie off at Nan's"

"No need," replied my uncle, "since Yoshiko is going to keep him, she needs to meet him and start spending some time with him. You only got a week before you ship out to Vietnam and Yoshiko needs this time to starting bonding with Freddy so that when you leave, he won't be uncomfortable with her."

"But, Nan will still be around to help out," replied my father.

"Not as much Doug. You don't want Freddie to pull away from Yoshiko when he sees Nan," replied my uncle.

The last of the fighter planes had finished their maneuvers as my uncle, father and I left the apartment complex heading out toward the main gate and into the village. The glow of the rising moon greeted the sun as it settled beyond the horizon- villagers were closing their shops as fishing boats were returning from the sea, preparing to unload their day's catch. The sounds of barking dogs filled the air as the evening beetle bugs began to sing their mating calls attracting the bug catchers who made their living capturing these bugs and selling them at the markets as delightful appetizers. My uncle had pulled his jeep into the muddy driveway, which led to Mr. Tokumori's wooded lot. My uncle had described Mr. Tokumori's house as meager with 3 rooms and a small kitchen with a detached bathroom in the backyard. There were a couple of old rusted bicycles on the front porch as the trio of my uncle, father and I, made our way to the front door. My uncle knocked loudly on the cedar- wooded front door noticing the craftsmanship and artistry designs embedded in the door.

"Very nice door," my Uncle Gill said, as he waited for someone to open the door from the other side.

"No doubt," replied my father agreeing with my uncle's assessment of the door.

The voice on the other side was gentle and meek as Mr. Tokumori opened the door and greeted everyone in Japanese. He had invited us to sit at the kitchen table as he poured hot tea for my father and uncle along with some crab and shrimp tempura appetizers that he had freshly prepared. Mr. Tokumori had explained to my father and uncle that his daughter, Yoshiko, would be arriving shortly. The men ate and drank as a giant aquarium full of fish and other sea life kept me fascinated. My uncle had confirmed with Mr. Tokumori that everything was taken care of including all of his stipulations concerning payment and the safe return of Yoshiko back to Okinawa, which my father reaffirmed. The anticipation of Yoshiko's arrival filled my father's body with anxiety, as his eyes wandered back and forth from the front door to the ticking of a clock hanging on a nearby wall. My uncle did most of the conversing with Mr. Tokumori knowing that my father was preoccupied with thoughts of meeting Yoshiko. My father was looking at family photographs placed in different locations of the front room and in the kitchen when a knocking sound caught the attention of all three men.

"That must be Yoshiko," said Mr. Tokumori speaking in Japanese. He had politely excused himself from the table and swiftly made his way to open the front door.

"Just relax Doug," my uncle said in a reassuring tone to my father.

After a short exchange of greetings between Yoshiko and her father, Mr. Tokumori returned to where my uncle and father were sitting in the kitchen.

This is my father's account of what took place:

"I don't know why I was so nervous. I could feel the nausea in my intestines pushing crap through my stomach- it was like a chorus of bubbles passing gas in the air as I tried to keep myself calm. Within the next few days, I would be marrying this woman that I would meet for the first time and more importantly, would become a mother to my son. How would little Freddie react to Yoshiko and how would she react to him was my top concern. From my conversation with Mr. Tokumori, this was strictly a business arrangement for him that would allow him to expand his fishing business as well as give his daughter some military benefits. When I heard what sounded like a lite tap at the door, I felt my heart drop to my stomach and looked at Gill for some words of encouragement. He told me to calm down and be cool. Mr. Tokumori made his way back to the kitchen, but without Yoshiko present. I asked Mr. Tokumori if something was wrong, but he said everything was fine. I whispered to Gill that I didn't see Yoshiko and wondered if everything was ok. Mr. Tokumori must have read my mind as he spoke out that Yoshiko was in the front room area playing with my son. Gill and I had gotten up and followed Mr. Tokumori to the front room where I was astonished and surprised to see Yoshiko and my son playing and talking. Little Freddie was repeating in Japanese all the names of the fishes that Yoshiko had just taught him. It seem that he bonded to her instantly as he sat in her lap pointing and naming each fish that swam in front of them. Seeing this brought relief to my anxieties and ease the bubbling action taking place in my stomach. Mr. Tokumori threw me a glace of approval as he led us down the hallway to the back gazebo area surround by Japanese Lily plants. My uncle Gill had pointed out that Captain Williams had made all the necessary arrangements for my father to marry Yoshiko within the next 24 hours before he was to be deployed to Vietnam. After all three men had agreed on the stipulations and the initial payoff completed, my father made his way back to the front room of the house where he observed Yoshiko holding me on her lap singing Japanese nursery rhymes.

"Looks like they're going to be good for each other," said my uncle Gill as he smiled toward my father.

"Yeah, looks like it. I just hope Freddie will adjust to his new environment," replied my father.

"They'll be fine. We better get a move on Doug- tomorrow's your big day," my uncle Gill said with a grin.

Mr. Tokumori accompanied both men outside as all three men exchanged final customary bows. Yoshiko had brought me to my father as she bided him farewell. My father, not knowing what to do, took Yoshiko's hand and gently kissed it.

My mother, Yoshiko, gave me this account of her reaction of what transpired at the time:

"My father had discussed with me a deal that he had made with the American military men involving me getting married and taking care of a little boy. I was totally against it and had been arguing with my father the entire day. I didn't want to leave Okinawa to go to the United States. I've heard a lot of bad things about the American people and their weird customs. My father said that money was too valuable and I would be well taken care of and flown back to Okinawa. We needed the money and my father promised that all would be fine. I was very nervous in meeting these American Army men and that I did all I could to stay out late in hoping that I would miss seeing them. I arrived home and my heart sank as I saw the jeep parked outside. I had quietly knocked and opened the door gently, creeping inside slowly as to not make any noise that would grab their attention. I heard my father talking with strange men when I felt a tug at my coat. I looked down and saw a little toddler pulling me toward the aquarium. He was pointing to each fish that swam by as I would call out the names and he repeated every name. After the first few minutes, he was naming all the fishes as they swam by. I was so impressed that I didn't notice my father and the other two men with him. My father had called out to me and gestured for me to come and meet the company. Nervousness overtook my entire being as I tried to speak but all I could do was nod my head and bow. I didn't know what to say. I went back to playing with the little boy as my father and the two men were talking amongst each other. This was my first encounter up close with a black man and I was very much afraid of going through the arrangement that my father agreed to. I didn't know what my father was getting us into."

Mr. Tokumori and Yoshiko waved good-bye as my uncle and father, with me on his lap, drove away heading back toward the base.

"Not bad at all," my uncle said as he was lighting his cigar. A silent look filled my father's face as he kept looking in the side view mirror catching the last waving glimpse of Yoshiko.

"Yes, not bad at all- it may just work out Gill." My father had later said that he thought Yoshiko was more beautiful than he had originally thought and her humbleness attracted him to her.

Chapter 36

THE RESOUNDING RUMBLES OF FIGHTER jets made their way across Naha Air Base as my father was putting on his uniform thinking about Yoshiko and the marriage that would take place. His thoughts had him stuck in a dazed trance as he was looking in the mirror wondering if getting married to Yoshiko was the right thing to do. All that mattered was that he would be able to get his son back to the states and send Yoshiko back to her father. But first, he would have to survive the horrors of Vietnam, which were only a few days away.

"Hey Doug," shouted my uncle Gill coming through the unlocked door. "It's about that time. Captain Williams will be waiting for us."

"I'm coming man," replied my father. "Are you sure this is the thing to do Gill?"

"Yeah, giving the circumstance- everything will be fine." The positive reassurance from Gill still left my father's stomach fluttering with butterflies as they both walked out and took the jeep headed for Captain William's office.

The skies above Naha were littered with fighter planes and bombers going on maneuvers in preparing for their entrance into Vietnam. The base had been on full alert since the visit of General Westmoreland, who was in charge of executing the U.S. military forces into the Vietnam War. A fresh load of soldiers had just arrived and would be deploying to Vietnam along with my father in a couple of days. My uncle and my father noticed a black soldier walking by himself toward the Post Exchange store. My father had motioned for Gill to stop and offer a ride.

"Hey private, need a ride?" asked my father. The private, upon seeing my father and uncle, stood at attention.

"Sir, no sir," replied the private nervously.

"It's ok private. You don't have to be formal with us son," replied Gill as he extended his hand. "What's your name son?"

"Private First Class Desmond Wilson, sir."

"Ok, Private Wilson. I'm Sergeant Gill and this is Sergeant Douglas. If we can help you out with anything, let us know."

"Yes sir," replied Private Wilson. He was an unknown soldier at the time fighting for his country, but Private Desmond Wilson would later become an actor and entertainer appearing in one of my father's favorite T.V. series as Lamont Sanford of the show *"Sanford and Son."*

Mr. Tokumori and Yoshiko were waiting in Captain Williams's office along with two other Japanese Officials when my Uncle Gill and my father entered.

"Gill, Doug- just in time," said Captain Williams. He went on to explain that the two Japanese officials were "paid" by the Army for private services rendered on different occasions. They were there to officially file the marriage to the Japanese government without having any questions asked and any investigations stopped. My father had noticed that Yoshiko was looking as beautiful as ever with her hair twisted up into a ball and wore a two piece skirt set that fitted her nicely. After all introductions had been formally made, Captain Williams instructed everyone to have a seat as a set of documents were being distributed to each person. Captain Williams then gave a nod to one of the Japanese officials and he began to read the entirety of the documents in Japanese. Afterwards, Captain Williams re-read the same documents in English.

This is my father's account of what was going on at this time:

"The set up in Captain Williams's office wasn't what I was expecting when Gill and I entered the office. I thought that a chaplain would be there to perform the standard marriage ceremony and I would slip on the ring and give Yoshiko a kiss which I was kind of looking forward. Mr. Tukomori, Yoshiko and the two distinguished Japanese looking men were sitting around a table when Gill and I walked in. Captain Williams greeted us and introduced us to everyone as we all shook hands and sat at our assigned seats. Captain Williams then passed out a binder of documents as he nodded to one of the Japanese men to read. Not really understanding fully what was being said in Japanese, Captain Williams then read the same documents in English. The document precisely outlined the terms and conditions of the marriage as well an attached marriage certificate. Captain Williams then directed everyone to affix their signatures on the appropriate pages as the documents were rotated around the table. I was looking through the pages still confused about what was going on and I looked over at Gill and gave him a 'What the hell is going on look?' Gill sensed my reluctance and asked Captain Williams if we could have a private moment with him outside of his office."

"What's going on Doug, Gill?" asked Captain Williams as he closed the door behind him.

"We're both confused about what's going on. We thought the chaplain was supposed to be here," replied my uncle Gill as he threw a glance of agreement toward my father.

"Well actually, because of the complexity of the situation, I had to change the plan to avoid any questions being asked. The two Japanese men you see are actually Japanese government officials that we pay money to give us information and or reports that would be of interest to us."

"You mean they're spies?!" asked my father.

"Not exactly. They're more like our liaisons to the Japanese government to help with cutting through a lot of red tape to get things done."

"And you pay them to do whatever it is?" asked my father.

"Kind of sorts," replied Captain Williams. "Anyway, all we have to do is sign the documents and they will be filed with the Japanese government as well with our agencies here and in the U.S."

"So, just signing these documents will make the marriage official? asked my uncle Gill beating my father to the same question.

"Yes. The marriage between Doug and Yoshiko will be official," replied Captain Williams.

"Wow, that's crazy," said my father as he threw a questioning glance at my uncle Gill. "Damn, Captain. Makes me wonder what else our government can do under the table."

"You would be shocked if you knew only half the story about our government cover-ups," remarked Captain Williams.

Looking at his watch, Captain Williams quickly explained all the nuances of all the documents and why things were being done this way-mainly to protect the illegal rescue operation and all those involved. After all the questions were answered, the three men returned back to the office and upon instruction from Captain Williams, affixed their signatures to the appropriate signature lines. After all the signing was complete, Captain Williams stood up and formally introduced Mr. Tokumori's daughter as Mrs. Yoshiko Douglas. There was a short applause as Yoshiko, at the urging of her father, stood by my father's side. Taking Yoshiko's left hand, my father slipped on a gold wedding band on her ring finger and gently kissed her on the cheek. Just like that, they were husband and wife in less than a week after meeting each other.

Carrying sealed stuffed envelopes, Captain Williams had escorted the two Japanese men out of the office and presented the envelopes to them and bided them farewell. Mr. Tokumori briefly spoke to both my uncle Gill and my father about the arrangements to have Freddie Jr. dropped off to Yoshiko. My father would grabbed me from Nancy's and bring me along with all of my clothes and toys to Mr. Tokumori's home later that evening. My father would be leaving for Vietnam in less than 48 hours and wanted to give his son time to adjust to Yoshiko and his new environment. My father would spend a few hours getting to know Yoshiko and Mr. Tokumori. He wanted to make sure that they were comfortable having a toddler running around their home and that his son would respond favorably to his new environment.

Silence of a Friend

Sometimes silence between two friends
Are worth a thousand words
Just to have the presence of their comfort
Helps give the soul a peaceful mind
And eases painful piercings of the heart

He listens to the hurt in my voice
And shares my tears with every cry
He struggles to see the agony in my eyes
And feels the confusion in my blank stares
Asking himself how he can relieve my suffering

Each word he speaks brings forth encouragement
Helps to comfort to my broken heart
He extend his hand to lift me up
And carries my burdens for many miles
He never thinks of himself or his needs

His footsteps for me are priceless
He endures the shamefulness of my pity
Never once does he allow me to fall
He's always there even when I don't ask
No matter how far or time of day

His friendship has no price in life
As he would sacrifice his life for mine
This kind of friend is rare indeed
Who tells the truth no matter the pain
His advice brings healing to any situation

He always gave without being asked
Never seeking anything in return
He doesn't accuse or place blame
But always says, "I got your back"
I thank you, my friend, for being there for me.

Chapter 37

THE SUN WAS SETTING ON Norfolk Street when Captain Williams mentioned that it was time for him to take his daily walk to Charlie's Food Store and get his broiled peanuts and devil crabs. He had become familiar with Charlie and his family, especially the cashier, Jessie, who knew him by name and always greeted him with a smile.

"C"mon Smitty, take a walk with me and get some exercise- I'll buy you a devil crab."

"I guess so," replied Smitty. "I need to stretch my legs anyway."

The two men exited out of the front door and started on their way to Charlie's. It was a usual hot sunny day in Tampa as a stilled breeze swept lightly through the River Grove neighborhood. Across the street from our house was a large birch tree that had covered both sides of Norfolk Street, which provided a cool calm shade with nestled birds and chattering squirrels making their evening time food rounds. Sgt. Johnson and Sgt. Rolly took a few minutes to catch some sleep on the lawn chairs under the tree shade as my father and Uncle Gill were chatting with the next door neighbors about their fresh catch of fish from the day. As usual, my mother was at the flea market stocking up on household goods and talking with friends. I was in the house watching episodes of 'Happy Days" on T.V. when I heard my Uncle calling me.

"Yes Sir," I replied to the sound of my uncle's voice.

"How about taking me to get some cigars in Ybor City. I like to stock up before we leave on Sunday."

"Yes sir, I can do that."

At that moment, it had dawned on me that everyone would be leaving in a couple of days- I was enjoying myself listening to the close knit group of men telling their stories as I had grown accustomed to them and hated to know they would soon be leaving, going back to their separate lives. I had enjoyed spending time with them listening to their own personal stories and engaging conversations about life itself. I would soon be off to college in New Orleans attending Dillard University, taking the pride and spirit of these men with me.

My uncle and I were riding down 22nd street listening to the Doobie Brothers on my new dynamic sounding speakers, singing along with the background singers. The sign quickly approach that read, "entering Ybor City." For those of you that don't know about Ybor City, here is a little background:

Ybor City is a historic neighborhood in Tampa, Florida located just northeast of downtown. It was founded in the 1880s by cigar manufacturers and was populated by thousands of immigrants, mainly from Spain, Cuba, and Italy. For the next 50 years, workers in Ybor City's cigar factories would roll millions of cigars annually. The neighborhood had features unusual among contemporary immigrant communities in the southern United States, most notably its multi-ethnic and multi-racial population and their many mutual aid societies. A slow exodus out of the area that began during the Great Depression accelerated after World War II, leading to a period of abandonment and decay. After decades of neglect, a portion of the original neighborhood has redeveloped into a night club and entertainment district.

The neighborhood has been designated as a National Historic Landmark District, and several structures in the area are listed in the National Register of Historic Places. In 2008, 7th Avenue, the main commercial thoroughfare in Ybor City, was recognized as one of the "10 Great Streets in America" by the American Planning Association. In the early 1880s, Tampa was an isolated village with a population of less than 1000 and a struggling economy. However, its combination of a good port, Henry Plant's new railroad line, and humid climate attracted the attention of Vicente Martinez Ybor, a prominent Spanish-born cigar manufacturer. Ybor had moved his cigar-making operation from Cuba to Key West, Florida in 1869, due to political turmoil in the then-Spanish colony. But, labor unrest and the lack of room for expansion had him looking for another base of operations, preferably in his own company town. Ybor considered several communities in the southern United States and decided that an area of sandy scrubland just northeast of Tampa would be the best location. In 1885, the Tampa Board of Trade helped broker an initial purchase of 40 acres of land, and Ybor quickly bought more. Cigar making was a specialized trade, and Tampa did not possess a workforce able to man the new factories. To attract employees, Ybor built hundreds of small houses for the coming influx of mainly Cuban and Spanish cigar workers, many of whom followed him from Key West and Cuba. Other cigar manufacturers, drawn by incentives provided by Ybor to further increase the labor pool, also moved in, and quickly were making Tampa a major cigar production center.

After leaving Ybor City with his newly purchased box of Cuban cigars, my uncle asked about going to the mall and picking up some gifts for his kids back home in Texas.

"Sure, uncle, I can take you to Tampa Bay Center- it's by the stadium where the Buccaneers play"

"Oh yeah, The Tampa Bay Bucs. You know they lost 16 straight games before winning a game."

"Yeah, I know. Our first win was against the New Orleans Saints," I said.

"If I remember correctly," my uncle said as if he was in deep thought, "Tampa Bay almost made it to the Superbowl a couple of years ago with Doug Williams as their quarterback."

Doug Williams was one of the first black quarterbacks in the NFL drafted from Grambling University by the Tampa Bay Bucs- he eventually left Tampa after being labeled as a mindless QB who couldn't take his team to the next level; how ironic in that he led the Washington Redskins to a Superbowl and won.

As we pulled into the parking area of Tampa Bay Center, my uncle was reading the directional signs showing where certain stores were located inside the mall.

"I've never heard of some of these stores: Maas Brothers, Burdines, Montgomery Ward- the only one I recognize is JC Penny."

"They're all about the same. Some more expensive than others," I replied.

My uncle had agreed as we walked through the mall looking at various store fronts not really stopping to look around in any of them. We had come across a 'Spencer's Gift Shop' which had a lot of gag gifts which my uncle bought plenty.

"A lot of crazy stuff," my uncle said.

After spending about an hour shopping, we decided to head back to the house and catch up with the others.

The sound of the "Bee Gees" filled the air with their rendition of the song 'Staying Alive" as my uncle and I pulled up into the driveway of the house. Captain Williams and Sgt. Smith were busy sitting in chairs by the side door feasting on broiled peanuts like they were going out of style. Captain Williams had ordered 10 large bags of broiled peanuts from Charlie's that he would pick up on his way to the airport on Sunday for his return trip to Texas. My mother had just returned from the Flea Market with her usual assortment of household goods that she always purchased regardless if the closets were overflowing with the items she bought weekly. There was no sign of the others or my father and I had asked Captain Williams where they had went. I was anxious to get on with the story of what happened with my mother, Yoshiko, and me as well as with my father during the Vietnam War. Captain Williams said that my father and the others went to the 'ABC' liquor store to purchase some more beers and alcohol. My mother had started frying the fresh 'Mullet' fish that she had bought from the 40th Street Seafood Store for the group of men to eat during the coming night.

The smell of fish permeated through the air as loud voices and slamming car doors signaled the arrival of my father and the others.

"That fish smells good said my uncle Gill as he had pondered about who would eat a fish named "Mullet". After tasting the 'Mullet', my uncle Gill took a whole piece of the fish out of the oven and proceeded to do an expert oral ingestion of fresh cooked fish. My mother had laid out the food on the table as the others soon join in the fish parade commenting how good it tasted. Pabst Blue Ribbon, Colt 45 and Old Milwaukee's Best line the table as each man was smacking their lips and eating the fish right down to the bone. My mother sat quietly in the den eating her fish while watching episodes of "The Jeffersons" and "All in the Family". The loud squeaky voice of Edith Bunker brought Capt. Williams into the den.

"Oh man, I love "All in the Family" said Capt. Williams. 'That Archie Bunker is a riot." He sat on the opposite chair from my mother watching the show.

My uncle Gill had gone outside to smoke one of his fresh Cuban cigars while observing the evening sunset bringing the day slowly to a close. My father had joined him with a couple of Colt 45's beers while the others were still eating.

"So far, so good," said my father referring to how the stories were unfolding.

"Yep. We got a couple of days to wrap it all up before we all leave. I at least want to visit MacDill once more before we leave," replied my Uncle, referring to the Air Force Base.

"We can probably do MacDill on Saturday night since y'all will be leaving on Sunday. They got their seafood and barbeque buffet at the NCO club."

"Sounds good to me. I'm sure the others would look forward to going and having one last get together. I wish that the whole unit could have gotten together and shared this moment in time with us," my Uncle said as he gazed at the rising orange moon while sipping on his beer. A moment of silence fell between the two best friends as they both felt a huge burden being lifted off their shoulders.

"You know Gill, it feels good to get all of this off our chest," said my father as the crickets nearby chirped in unison.

"Yeah, it does. I say we finish everything by tomorrow night – that way we can relax for a moment and prepare for MacDill," replied my Uncle Gill as circular puffs of smoke from his cigar invaded the evening air.

"I'm good with that. I'll get the others together and we can pick up in a few," my father replied as he went inside the house. My uncle had stayed outside for a moment to watch the twinkling lights of a 747 passing overhead into the evening horizon. A warm gentle breeze caressed his face as though a divine presence had touched him and for the first time in many years, he felt at peace. A lonely teardrop made its way down his face as he gave thanks to God- he toasted his beer to the sky and finished the remainder of his cigar. This is my Uncle's account of what he was experiencing at this time:

I thought about what we all went through and how amazing it was that we were all able to survive to get to this point in time. I was reminiscing back through the years and realized how bless we all were when it all hit me at once; I finally came to the realization that something greater had kept us all together to bring us to this point in time. I was never a big believer in spiritual things, but I knew that Divine Hands played a big role. That's when calmness came over me to confirm my thoughts. Seeing Freddy Jr. grow up and to be here celebrating 18 years of life is a miracle within itself considering what he went through and all the adversities he had to face- I thanked God, giving Him the Glory, for this was truly a miracle."

The rest of the guys were inside talking about the debut of MTV on cable, the rising gasoline prices which was steady at $1.15 per gallon and the possibility of an air traffic controllers strike, which President Reagan held a news conference threatening to terminate any air traffic controller who joins in the strike. Major League Baseball had recently ended their strike and it didn't hold too well with sports fans across the nation since they all talked about boycotting the games to show baseball players their disappointment. My father was sorting through his stack of 45's (music records for those who weren't around when music was recorded on vinyl plastic disc with a hole in the middle) pulling out records to play on his RCA record player. King Floyd's "Grove Me Baby" blasted through the speakers as my father and Uncle started dancing and "bumping" each other. The others got up and joined in as my mom and I laugh heartily- it was funny seeing a bunch of old dudes trying to dance.

"What you know about this?!" shouted Sgt. Smitty as he was doing some sort of robotic dance.

"Man, that ain't nothing. Catch a little bit of this funky chicken," replied Captain Williams as he was jerking his head and flapping his elbows with his arms tucked in.

But the funniest dance went to Sgt. Rolly when he "popped" and "snapped" his body with George Clinton's "Atomic Dog" playing in the background. You could hear the cracking of bones as he tried to contort his body in different directions and pulled a hamstring muscle.

"Whew, that's enough," said Sgt. Johnson as he flopped himself down on the couch. The others agreed as they joined him on the couch trying to catch their breath in unison. It was a sight to behold as my mom and I laughed the entire time. This was truly a "Kodak" picture perfect moment that would become priceless.

An hour had passed when my Uncle Gill asked if they wanted to call it the night or continue on telling the stories of Vietnam as it pertained to my father and me.

"I think we need to call it the night," said my father pointing to Capt. Williams and Sgt. Johnson, both of whom were trying to out snore each other.

"I guess so. We can probably meet up tomorrow for breakfast in the morning," replied my Uncle Gill.

"Yeah, how about that pancake place by Busch Gardens," asked Sgt. Smith. "The one we passed the other day going to the VA hospital."

"You're talking about the Village Inn," replied my mother.

"Yeah, that's it. I've been having a taste for strawberry banana pancakes," said Sgt. Smith as his mouth began to moisten with the thought of his craving.

A half hour later, after finalizing the plans for the next morning, I loaded the group into my car and headed back to the Admiral Benbow Inn for their night's rest. Before I could even get to the hotel, they were all knocked out and snoring like donkeys. It was an honor for me to be with these men who risked their lives not only for me, but for their country as well, even though their country didn't take care of them the way it should have. After dropping off Capt. Williams and Sgt. Smitty to their rooms, I decided that I still had time to go by one of my closest friend and see what he was doing.

"What up?" I shouted at Otto, giving him dap with the hands.

"Nothing much man, just watching some Bruce Lee flicks. Haven't seen you in a while- what's been up?" replied Otto.

"Just entertaining some guests from out of town."

Otto Strickland Jr. and I had become close friends while attending Hillsborough High School and we had labeled ourselves as "Nighthawks" after the movie starring Sylvester Stallone and Carl Weathers. Otto and I would see very little of each other as he was preparing to attend the University of South Florida and I was leaving for Dillard University in New Orleans. We would lose contact with each other as the years progressed.

"Some of my father's military buddies came into town to share my 18th birthday and spend some time with the family," I said.

"That sounds cool. That your ride?" asked Otto.

"Yep, one of my birthday gifts."

Otto was surveying the car as I threw him the keys to start it up.

"Nice," said Otto cranking up the volume on the stereo blasting "Planet Rock" through my newly amplified speakers. "Sweet sound system."

After a few moments of listening to the music, the porch lights from Otto's house flickered off and on. "Oops, better turn down the music bro," said Otto, telling me that the flickering of the porch lights was a signal to that the music was too loud.

"We ought to hook up this weekend and do a little something," I said. "My father's company will be gone after Saturday. Maybe we can get together on Sunday or one day next week."

"Sounds good to me bro. We can ride out to USF and check out the campus and the chicks."

"That's a bet." After a few more moments of conversing and setting up plans, I gave Otto a hugging handshake and departed for home.

My mother was busy at the sewing machine like a mad scientist stitching together a pants suit from a pattern she bought at the flea market. She was very talented; she made most of her clothes that she wore, but she was especially known for the exquisite Japanese pillow patterns that she made for neighbors, friends and family members. She was one never to charge money for making her pillows for others, but if she did, she could have easily made an extra five hundred dollars or more per month. I could hear "Here's Johnny" coming from the TV as the Johnny Carson show was coming on and my father and Uncle Gill were both sleep, still clutching beer cans in their hands. My father had on a tank top tee shirt which had risen up above his bulging stomach up toward his chest. I could clearly see the permanent scars of war drawn like a map on his stomach. There was a wide fading gash on the right side of his stomach area where he had been stabbed deeply along with scarred indentations on the front of his stomach where enemy bullets made their presence known in the history of a wounded soldier. There was also surgical scar around the bullet holes- my guess was that surgery was needed to remove the bullets that penetrated his stomach. But the one wound that I couldn't take my eyes off was the large keloid gash where once a knife entered deeply during a certain rescue operation of a father looking for his son. All these years I saw that scar, but never knew how he got it. He never discussed it nor did I question him about it. But now, the pieces were starting to come together as I slowly understood who I am: I am my father's son.

Chapter 38

THE WAITRESS COULDN'T BELIEVE HER eyes as she brought another round of pancakes to the table. She had never seen anyone go through the initial stack of pancakes and then order more. Sgt.'s Smith and Johnson were thoroughly enjoying themselves eating to their hearts content like it was their last meal, even licking the warm maple syrup off of their fingers. Capt. Williams was reading the history of the Village Inn and noted that George Steinbrenner, owner of the New York Yankees, was a frequent visitor of the restaurant. Mr. Dow Sherwood opened his first Village Inn in 1961 in Tampa. It became his hangout. It also became the breakfast place for Tampa business people and politicians, for tourists, for the Cincinnati Reds, and for New York Yankees owner George Steinbrenner, who loved the pancakes and maple syrup, and felt that way about Mr. Sherwood too. I had to count about 15 pancakes was consumed by Sgt.'s Smith and Johnson and even Capt. Williams got in on the pancake feast eating about a dozen himself.

After everyone had finished their breakfasts, my father had decided to take them over to the Tampa Greyhound Track to catch the early matinee of the dog races. Opened in 1933, Tampa Greyhound Track is one of the oldest American greyhound racetracks. Every year, they run more than 3,000 races, entertain more than a half-million fans and give away some $100-million in winnings. The dog track was one of my father's favorite past times, considering the fact that his betting methods were very unusual. He was never the one to study the statistics of each dog as outlined in the dog racing program books or even look at the dogs when they were being introduced. My father would just go up to a betting window and bet 2 dollar trifectas on all 12 races picking out random numbers which didn't have any reasoning or logic behind them. Whatever 3 numbers came to his mind is what he betted and the funny thing is he would usually win at least 1 race out of 12 earning him from 20 to 500 dollars. The excitement of the crowd stirred as the track announcer shouted, "Here comes Rusty," which was a mechanical rabbit that led the dogs around the track to the finish line. All the other men, except for my Uncle Gill, acted like children at a carnival running along trackside to see which dogs crossed the finished line first. Their scientific logical formulas netted them zero dollars while my father walked out with 120 dollars on senseless bets.

"Hey Doug, you lucky son of a gun, how did you know that the 1-7-8 was going to come out in the last race?" asked Capt. Williams as we were headed back to our cars in the parking lot of the dog track.

"Lucky guess. Just pick those numbers out of the air," replied my father as he recouped the money he spent at breakfast picking up the entire tab.

Capt. Williams, Sgt. Smith and Sgt. Johnson were riding with me while the rest rode with my father as we headed back to Norfolk Street.

"Hey Freddy!" said Capt. Williams as we were riding down Sligh Ave. approaching the railroad tracks by Charlie's Food Store. I had already known that Capt. Williams was going to ask me to stop at Charlie's.

"I know Capt. Williams. I'm pulling in."

Sgt. Williams and Sgt. Johnson accompanied Capt. Williams inside the store while I stood outside taking time to observe the surroundings. It was a clear crisp cloudless day as birds lined across the telephone cable in front of Charlie's waiting for someone to drop some peanuts or pieces of food on the ground. The distant whistle of a train could be heard as patrons were standing around discussing various topics of the day and gossiping about what was going around the neighborhood. Every few minutes cars would drive by honking their horns and drivers waving to the familiar faces in the crowd or calling out names. Charlie's Food Store had become a staple in the community and through the years have seen the neighborhood children grow and bring their children to Charlie's to get a pack of Now and Later's candy or a pack of bubblegum. Charlie was amazing in that he knew everyone in the neighborhood by name and through many changes including the passing of Charlie, his family still runs the business today keeping the same values and trusts that keeps it thriving today. If you're ever in Tampa, go down Sligh Ave and stop in at Charlie's, located by the Tampa Electric Company. Try their broiled peanuts, deviled crabs and home cooked meals while chatting with Jesse and the family of Charlie's.

Loud laughing voices caught my attention as Capt. Williams came out with an armful of broiled peanuts and deviled crabs. Sgt.'s Smith and Johnson also had their share of broiled peanuts, jars of pickled pig's feet and a pile of lottery scratch tickets. My father had blew his horn as he and the others riding with him shouted out of the Cartier Edition Lincoln Mark V, which was my father's pride and joy. The oversized Lincoln was the first luxury car he ever owned as he was always up every morning wiping off the bird residue and other dirty spots around the car. My mother didn't particular care for the car because it was too long to drive and she rather drove her compact Datsun sedan.

The overcast skies had suggested a hint of rain was coming as we all unloaded the cars and headed into the house ready for the final day of stories to be told by the group of old soldiers. The noise of the sewing machine could be heard in the den as my mother was busy stitching together fabric making another of her signature outfits. The theme from 'Star Trek" was playing on the TV as everyone took their places in the living room as my father passed out the Colt 45's and Pabst Blue Ribbon beers. Capt. Williams opened up a couple of bags of broiled peanuts and poured them into a large bowl for everyone to enjoy.

"Thanks Doug, we all had a great time, especially at the dog track. It still amazes me how you pick out numbers with no logic behind it and still win," said Capt. Williams.

"It's just luck. I do the same thing for Jai- aLai," my father replied.

"Jai-aLai?" replied Capt. Williams as he never heard of the game.

"Yeah, Jai alai is a sport involving a ball bounced off a walled space. It's a ball game that originated in Spain's Basque region and is played in a three-walled court with a hard rubber ball that is caught and thrown with a cesta, a long, curved wicker scoop strapped to one arm. You bet on the teams who can outplay their opponents. You just have to see it," said my Uncle Gill.

After going over the game of Jai alai, my Uncle Gill suggested that they commence with the story if they wanted to stay on track to be finished. They were all looking at getting together at MacDill on Saturday night for one last night of eating and drinking along with having a lot of fun.

FREDERICK DOUGLAS, JR.

"Freddy, c'mon man, we're waiting on you," yelled my Uncle Gill.

"Coming," I said as I was watching the last segment of Captain Kirk and the Enterprise battle the Romulans on an episode of 'Star Trek".

"C'mon Scotty, we need more power," said Captain Kirk.

"I'm trying sir, I'm giving her all she's got," replied Scotty in his Scottish accent. In the end, Captain Kirk and the Enterprise always pulled through.

"So, where did we leave off?" asked my Uncle Gill as he motioned toward me to look in my notes which I had been taking.

"Yoshiko and Doug had gotten married and he was about to depart for Vietnam in less than 24 hours."

Chapter 39

THE ARRANGEMENTS WOULD BE THAT Yoshiko would keep little Freddy while Doug was away in Vietnam, giving them a chance to bond together. My Uncle Gill and Nurse Nan would serve as a backup if anything happened with Yoshiko for whatever reason.

This is my Uncle Gill's account of what transpired during this time:

"Doug had less than 24 hours before he would be shipping out to Vietnam to join his platoon. Word had come back from the field that 4 men had been killed from his platoon and several others wounded. This had greatly concerned Doug because his men were under the leadership of a white lieutenant who didn't really care to be in charge of a black platoon. Doug knew his men well and to have this many causalities was a result of leadership putting his men in wrong positions and leaving them exposed as targets for the enemy. Doug was able to spend a few hours with Yoshiko and Freddie over at Mr. Tokumori's home and he started to grow fond of Yoshiko and wished he had more time to spend with her. Her humbleness attracted Doug as I recalled him saying that over and over. As for Freddy, he instantly bonded with Yoshiko and their relationship would flourish to the point of him knowing her as his mother."

Deafening jet engines and the roaring thunder of C130's filled the shiny blue skies over Naha Air Base as platoons of soldiers were being loaded ready for transport to the Vietnam war zone. The base commanders and members of the Joints Chiefs of Staffs were on hand to observe this next round of deployment into Vietnam War Theater. All the platoon leaders had been briefed on their assignments and now were ready to carry out their orders. This would be a joint deployment of over 30,000 men from the Marines, Air force, Army and Navy. My father was on board one of the C130 transports as he nervously thought about Vietnam and if he would make it back alive. He had left instructions with my Uncle Gill that if he didn't return alive, my uncle was to take me with him, leaving Yoshiko behind. He would be granted full parental guardianship and was to raise me like one of his own children. My Uncle Gill said that he was prepared to raise me and that it would be an honor for him to do it, especially for my father.

"Sgt. Douglas!" shouted one of the lieutenants, who my father described as looking like a 16 year old teenager. "We have a position on your platoon and the location where you will be joining them."

"Yes sir!" replied my father as the young lieutenant went over aerial and ground maps of the fight zone and where his platoon was stationed.

"Sgt., once we land in the safe zone and deplane, you will deploy with C Platoon and then once they get into this area, you will find your men here," said the lieutenant as he was pointing to different areas on the map. "They're expecting you."

My father nodded his approval giving the young lieutenant a salute as he started scanning the map for further details. He had said that the plane ride was gloomy as reports of casualties blackened the many thoughts of the men sitting side by side, reciting prayers.

This is my father's account of what was going on during this time:

The fear in the eyes of the young soldiers illuminated from the depts of their souls created a clear silence which one could hear a pin drop despite the roaring turbines of the C130 engines thundering through the skies. Maybe, there was just a glimmer of hope that the C130 would turn around and head back to Naha where they could all go back home. One of the soldiers cried silently as tears of anxiety trickled down his face as it displayed a horrified look that said, "I don't want to die." This was one of the few times where it didn't matter what race or color you were- this was a war that no one wanted to fight or die for. No matter what comforting words that the lieutenants were saying, the fact was that half of us wouldn't return alive. Many times I stared death in its face and told it to 'kiss off' and survived, but this time, death was waiting with an outstretched hand and I would have nowhere else to go. I closed my eyes and thought of Yoshiko and my son and determined that death would not get me this time either. This war wasn't about fighting for America, but fighting to survive and live so that all of us could return to our families and live somewhat of a normal life. I could see the fear gripping these young men's hearts- they were all very young, some just fresh out of basic training ready to defend their country or so they thought. There were just a handful of black soldiers as I could also see the looks of death on their faces as they seem to be looking at me for some glimmer of hope. I gave them a simple nod like that would reassure them everything would be ok- I knew that this could be the last time I would see any of them alive for demons were waiting for us on the battlefield. All I could think about was Yoshiko and my son and how I had to make it back alive. I also thought about my men and wondered how many of their lives were lost. If it wasn't for my men, I might have reconsidered Gill's idea of taking a medical exemption and avoid the Vietnam War. A crying voice caught my attention as I saw tears making its way down one of the faces of a young white soldier. He cried out, "I don't want to die, please take me back." One of the other sergeants quickly informed the crying soldier that he was a U.S. Army soldier fighting for his country and tried to reassure him that he wouldn't die. A few of the soldiers would spend the plane ride writing letters to their love ones while others tried to sleep. All I could do was think and recount my life through the years hoping to leave a memory or two of who I am so that my son would know something about his father. I hadn't plan on dying but just in case, I wanted to make sure my son knew that I was his father and I loved him."

Chapter 40

AFTER LANDING IN VIETNAM AND deploying to their assigned areas, my father had entered a war torned village as the first sign of reality of death filled his nostrils from the dozens and dozens of decaying bodies and body parts laying on top of one another. The blood of men, women and children filled the dirt roads and their cries could still be heard coming from the ground. My father knelt down at the body of a young child and tears came down my father's face as he thought about the future this child would never have. "Damn, this is some messed up stuff. What are we doing in this war?" my father thought to himself as he laid a nearby blanket over the dead child.

Violent eruptions of bombs could be heard and felt as the platoons scrambled northward toward the action. My father had caught up with one of the platoon sergeants and inquired about their position and the enemy's location.

"We're about 4 miles from initial enemy contact and all reports we're getting doesn't look good- casualties are mounting," said the platoon sergeant as he continued receiving reports. "Your platoon should be somewhere along this path that we're following."

The stench of torn bodies could be smelled from miles away as the wind carried the spirits of those that died to their temporary resting place awaiting their final judgment. The scenery was like a page out of hell with bloody demons scourging dead bodies for souls to take back to their master and claim a great reward. This would be the scene over and over as the Vietnam War continued and men gave their lives for a senseless cause to be justified by saying that our freedom was at risk. But, none the less, these men fought not for their country, but for their families. This is my father's recollection of one of those scenes:

"We had stumbled upon a partial village which had been pummeled by bombs and enemy gunfire. There was a wall that was left from a 2 story building which hanged six bodies of American soldiers that had been riddled with bullets from head to toe. It was as though whoever did this was using the bodies as target practice and who knows if these soldiers were alive or dead before being shot. One of the lieutenants went up to the bodies and noticed by the uniforms that they were three U.S. marines and 3 U.S. army soldiers. The bodies were decimated too badly to be saved for transport so we buried them on location. I knew then that if I survived this war, it would be by the Grace of God. This wasn't America's war, but Satan's war and we were interfering with it."

"Sgt. Douglas, I just received word that your platoon is waiting for you a couple of miles ahead," said one the lieutenants. Clouds of dark smoke could be seen from miles away as a barrage of bombs could be heard in the distance. My father had wondered how many men had died from his platoon and would they survive to see him.

"Thanks, sir," replied my father as he fell in formation with the others making their way toward the battle zone. The smell of death nauseated the stomachs of the men as they marched their way through, some covering up their noses to keep the stench of dead bodies and animals away from them. My father said that he felt like he was an ant in a graveyard- there were body parts everywhere being consumed by maggots and birds of prey. Scenes like these hadn't even begun to scratch the surface of what the U.S. armed forces would encounter during their tour of duty in Vietnam. My father eventually caught up with his men and it became an intense nine month battle against the Viet Cong and those factions that supported them. My father lost men whose bodies were never found and some were "damaged" for life, mentally and physically. Many still believe that this was a war that the United States should have never entered and that we will never know the truth behind Vietnam. As Capt. Williams said, "You be surprise at what our government can cover up."

Epilogue

AFTER MY FATHER RETURNED FROM Vietnam, it took him a while to find some sense of normalcy and restore his mind to some level of humanity. The nightmares from Vietnam would always continue to haunt him till his death, but at least, he made it back alive to see his son and wife. After a few months of medical treatments and psychological evaluations, my father was cleared to return to normal duty. Capt. Williams had arranged for my father to be stationed in El Paso, Texas along with my Uncle Gill, who was stationed in Abilene, Texas. Yoshiko and I bonded well together and she became the only mother I ever knew. My father and Yoshiko also bonded and fell in love and she decided to stay and take care of my father and me. My Uncle Gill and my father stayed closed throughout the years until my uncle's death in 1999. Capt. Williams kept in contact off and on and he passed in 2003. Sgt. Arthur Smith passed in 1988 from cancer linked to Agent Orange from the Vietnam War. The others, I have not heard from, but if they read this story and are still alive, I would love to hear from them. As for my father, he passed in 2004 and my mother, Yoshiko, passed shortly thereafter in 2006 from a broken heart after losing my father. They are both buried at the Florida National Cemetery located in Bushnell, Florida, which is dedicated to the men and women who served in the U.S. armed services. If you're ever in the area, stop by and pay your respects to these men and women, then visit gravesite 323B and say hello to my parents for me. They are both missed and I am my father's son.

About the Author

FREDERICK HELPED PAID HIS WAY through college as a greeting card writer and writing romantic poetry. He compares his writing style to that of Frank Peretti and Dan Brown. He is currently working on a dramatic action series about angels and is also studying Jewish theology and resides in Atlanta, Georgia with his wife, Ruby.

Printed in the United States
By Bookmasters